John McDougall

Saddle, Sled and Snowshoe

Pioneering on the Saskatchewan in the Sixties

John McDougall

Saddle, Sled and Snowshoe
Pioneering on the Saskatchewan in the Sixties

ISBN/EAN: 9783337250171

Printed in Europe, USA, Canada, Australia, Japan

Cover: Foto ©Andreas Hilbeck / pixelio.de

More available books at **www.hansebooks.com**

SADDLE, SLED AND SNOWSHOE:

PIONEERING ON THE SASKATCHEWAN,
IN THE SIXTIES.

BY

JOHN McDOUGALL,

Author of "Forest, Lake and Prairie: Twenty Years of Frontier
Life in Western Canada," etc.

WITH ILLUSTRATIONS BY J. E. LAUGHLIN.

TORONTO:
WILLIAM BRIGGS,
Wesley Buildings.

Montreal: C. W. COATES.   Halifax: S. F. HUESTIS.

1896.

ENTERED according to Act of the Parliament of Canada, in the year one thousand eight hundred and ninety-six, by WILLIAM BRIGGS, at the Department of Agriculture.

CONTENTS.

Chapter I.

Old Fort Edmonton—Early missionaries—Down the Saskatchewan by dog-train—Camp-fire experiences—Arrival at home—Daily occupations . . . 11

Chapter II.

A foraging expedition—Our hungry camp—A welcome feast—Dogs, sleds and buffalo bull in a tangle—In a Wood Cree encampment—Chief Child, Maskepetoon and Ka-kake—Indian hospitality—Incidents of the return trip 19

Chapter III.

Scarcity of food—The winter packet—Start for Edmonton for the eastern mails—A lonely journey—Arrive at Fort Edmonton—Start for home—Camping in a storm—Improvising a "Berlin"—Old Draffan—Sleeping on a dog-sled *en route*—A hearty welcome home 30

Chapter IV.

Trip to Whitefish Lake—Mr. Woolsey as a dog-driver—Rolling down a side hill—Another trip to Edmonton—Mr. O. B. as a passenger—Perils of travel by ice—Narrow escape of Mr. O. B.—A fraud exposed—Profanity punished—Arrival at Edmonton—Milton and Cheadle—Return to Victoria . . 41

CONTENTS.

Chapter V.

Mr. Woolsey's ministrations—An exciting foot-race—Building operations—Gardening—Stolen (?) buffalo tongues—Addled duck eggs as a relish—A lesson in cooking—A lucky shot—Precautions against hostile Indians 51

Chapter VI.

The summer brigade—With the brigade down the Saskatchewan—A glorious panorama—Meet with father and mother on the way to Victoria—Privations of travel—A buffalo crossing—Arrival at Victoria—A church building begun—Peter Erasmus as interpreter 60

Chapter VII.

In search of the Stoneys—An Indian avenger—A Sunday at Fort Edmonton—Drunken Lake carousals—Indian trails—Canyon of the Red Deer—I shoot my father—Amateur surgeons—Prospecting for gold—Peter gets "rattled"—A mysterious shot—Friends or foes?—Noble specimens of the Indian race—A "kodak" needed—Among the Stoneys—Prospecting for a mission site—A massacre of neophytes—An Indian patriarch—Back at Victoria again 66

Chapter VIII.

Provisions diminishing—A buffalo hunt organized—Oxen and Red River carts—Our "buffalo runners"—Meet with Maskepetoon—Maskepetoon shakes hands with his son's murderer—An Indian's strange vow—Instance of Indian watchfulness—"Who-Talks-Past-All-Things"—Come upon the buffalo—An exciting charge—Ki-you-ken-os races the buffalo—Peter's exciting adventure—Buffalo dainties—

CONTENTS.

PAGE

Return home—War parties—Indian curiosity—Starving Young Bull's "dedication feast"—Missionary labors 80

CHAPTER IX.

The fall fishing—A relentless tooth-ache—Prairie and forest fire—Attacked by my dogs—A run home—A sleepless night—Father turns dentist—Another visit to Edmonton—Welcome relief—Final revenge on my enemy 96

CHAPTER X.

Casual visitors—The missionary a "medicine man"—"Hardy dogs and hardier men"—A buffalo hunt organized—"Make a fire! I am freezing!"—I thaw out my companion—Chief Child—Father caught napping—Go with Mr. Woolsey to Edmonton—Encounter between Blackfeet and Stoneys—A "nightmare" scare—My passenger scorched—Rolling down hill—Translating hymns . . . 104

CHAPTER XI.

Visited by the Wood Stoneys—"Muddy Bull"—A noble Indian couple—Remarkable shooting—Tom and I have our first and only disagreement—A race with loaded dog-sleds—Chased by a wounded buffalo bull—My swiftest foot-race—Building a palisade around our mission home—Bringing in seed potatoes 117

CHAPTER XII.

Mr. Woolsey's farewell visit to Edmonton—Preparing for a trip to Fort Garry—Indians gathering into our valley—Fight between Crees and Blackfeet—The "strain of possible tragedy"—I start for Fort Garry—Joined by Ka-kake—Sabbath observance—A camp of Saulteaux—An excited Indian—I dilate on the numbers and resources of the white man—We pass Duck Lake—A bear hunt—"Loaded for b'ar"—A contest in athletics—Whip-poor-wills—Pancakes and maple syrup—Pass the site of Birtle—My first and only difference with Ka-kake - - 128

Chapter XIII.

Fall in with a party of "plain hunters"—Marvellous resources of this great country—A "hunting breed"—Astounding ignorance—Visit a Church of England mission—Have my first square meal of bread and butter in two years—Archdeacon Cochrane—Unexpected sympathy with rebellion and slavery—Through the White Horse Plains—Baptiste's recklessness and its punishment—Reach our destination—Present my letter of introduction to Governor McTavish—Purchasing supplies—"Hudson's Bay blankets"—Old Fort Garry, St. Boniface, Winnipeg, St. John's, Kildonan—A "degenerate" Scot—An eloquent Indian preacher—Baptiste succumbs to his old enemy—Prepare for our return journey 140

Chapter XIV.

We start for home—A stubborn cow—Difficulties of transport—Indignant travellers—Novel method of breaking a horse—Secure provisions at Fort Ellice—Lose one of our cows—I turn detective—Dried meat and fresh cream as a delicacy . . . 151

Chapter XV.

Personnel of our party—My little rat terrier has a novel experience—An Indian horse-thief's visit by night—I shoot and wound him—An exciting chase—Saved by the vigilance of my rat terrier—We reach the South Branch of the Saskatchewan—A rushing torrent—A small skin canoe our only means of transport—Mr. Connor's fears of drowning—Get our goods over 160

CONTENTS.

Chapter XVI.

A raft of carts—The raft swept away—Succeed in recovering it—Getting our stock over—The emotionless Scot unbends—Our horses wander away—Track them up—Arrive at Carlton—Crossing the North Saskatchewan—Homes for the millions—Fall in with father and Peter—Am sent home for fresh horses—An exhilarating gallop—Home again . . 172

Chapter XVII.

Improvements about home—Mr. Woolsey's departure—A zealous and self-sacrificing missionary—A travelling college—I feel a twinge of melancholy—A lesson in the luxury of happiness—Forest and prairie fire—Father's visit to the Mountain Stoneys—Indians gathering about our mission—Complications feared 182

Chapter XVIII.

Maskepetoon—Council gatherings—Maskepetoon's childhood—"Royal born by right Divine"—A father's advice—An Indian philosopher—Maskepetoon as "Peace Chief"—Forgives his father's murderer—Arrival of Rev. R. T. Rundle—Stephen and Joseph—Stephen's eloquent harangue—Joseph's hunting exploits—Types of the shouting Methodist and the High Church ritualist 193

Chapter XIX.

Muh-ka-chees, or "the Fox"—An Indian "dude"—A strange story—How the Fox was transformed—Mr. The-Camp-is-Moving as a magician . . . 207

Chapter XX.

Victoria becomes a Hudson's Bay trading post—An adventure on a raft—The annual fresh meat hunt organized—Among the buffalo—Oliver misses his shot and is puzzled—My experience with a runaway horse—A successful hunt—My "bump of locality" surprises Peter—Home again 217

Chapter XXI.

Father and I visit Fort Edmonton—Peter takes to himself a wife—Mr. Connor becomes school teacher—First school in that part of the country—Culinary operations—Father decides to open a mission at Pigeon Lake—I go prospecting—Engage a Roman Catholic guide—Our guide's sudden "illness"—Through new scenes—Reach Pigeon Lake—Getting out timber for building—Incidents of return trip . 228

Chapter XXII.

Another buffalo hunt—Visit Maskepetoon's camp—The old chief's plucky deed—Arrival of a peace party from the Blackfeet—A "peace dance"—Buffalo in plenty—Our mysterious visitor—A party of Blackfeet come upon us—Watching and praying—Arrive home with well-loaded sleds—Christmas festivities 237

Chapter XXIII.

We set out with Maskepetoon for the Blackfoot camp—A wife for a target—Indian scouts—Nearing the Blackfeet—Our Indians don paint and feathers—A picture of the time and place—We enter the Blackfoot camp—Three Bulls—Buffalo Indians—Father describes eastern civilization—The Canadian Government's treatment of the Indians a revelation—I am taken by a war chief as a hostage—Mine host and his seven wives—Bloods and Piegans—I witness a great dance—We leave for home—A sprained ankle—Arrival at the mission 254

Chapter XXIV.

We visit the Cree camp—I lose Maple and the pups—Find our Indian friends "pound-keeping"—The Indian buffalo pound—Consecrating the pound—Mr. Who-Brings-Them-In—Running the buffalo in—The herd safely coralled—Wholesale slaughter—Apportioning the hunt—*Finis* 271

ILLUSTRATIONS.

	PAGE
"I made a fire, and by melting snow boiled my kettle" . . . . . . *Frontispiece*	
"The dogs and sleds went sliding in around him" .	23
"There he sat, his eyes bulging out with fear" . .	48
"The discharge of shot, bounding from this, struck both father and his horse"	70
"To save my life I had to climb to the top of the staging"	99
"I got Tom up, and held him close over the fire" .	107
"I bounded from before him for my life" . . .	124
"I headed her out again into the lake" . . .	155
"I took deliberate aim, and fired at him" . . .	165
"We went at a furious rate on that swirling, seething, boiling torrent"	173
Rev. Thomas Woolsey	184
"Tying our clothes in bundles above our heads, we started into the ice-cold current" . . .	219
"Slapping his head, I turned his course to smooth ground"	224
"Maskepetoon calmly . . . took out his Cree Testament . . . and began to read" . . .	239
"This strange Indian, without looking at us, sang on"	247
"Slapped-in-the-Face, take that one"	279

SADDLE, SLED AND SNOWSHOE

CHAPTER I.

Old Fort Edmonton—Early missionaries—Down the Saskatchewan by dog-train—Camp-fire experiences—Arrival at home—Daily occupations.

In my previous volume, "Forest, Lake and Prairie," which closed with the last days of 1862, I left my readers at Fort Edmonton. At that time this Hudson's Bay post was the chief place of interest in the great country known as the Saskatchewan Valley. To this point was tributary a vast region fully six hundred miles square, distinguished by grand ranges of mountains, tremendous foot hills, immense stretches of plain, and great forests. Intersecting it were many mighty rivers, and a great number of smaller streams. Lakes, both fresh and alkaline, dotted its broad surface.

Over the entire length and breadth of this big domain coal seemed inexhaustible. Rich soil and magnificent pasturage were almost universal. But as yet there was no settlement. The peoples who inhabited the country were nomadic. Hunting, trapping, and fishing were their means of livelihood, and in all this they were encouraged by the great Company to whom belonged the various trading-posts scattered over the wide area, and of which Fort Edmonton was chief.

For the collecting and shipping of furs Edmonton existed. For this one definite purpose that post lived and stood and had its being. A large annual output of the skins and furs of many animals was its highest ambition. Towards this goal men and dogs and horses and oxen pulled and strained and starved. For this purpose isolation and hardship almost inconceivable were undergone. For the securing and bringing in to Edmonton of the pelts of buffalo and bear, beaver and badger, martin and musk-rat, fisher and fox, otter and lynx, the interest of everyone living in the country was enlisted. Thirteen different peoples, speaking eight distinct languages, made this post their periodic centre; and while at Edmonton was shown the wonderful tact and skill of the Hudson's Bay Company in managing contending tribes, yet nevertheless many a frightful massacre took place under the shadow of its walls.

This was the half-way house in crossing the continent. Hundreds of miles of wildness and isolation were on either hand. About midway between and two thousand feet above two great oceans—unique, significant, and alone, without telegraphic or postal communication—thus we found Fort Edmonton in the last days of the last month of the year 1862.

Edmonton had been the home of the Rev. R. T. Rundle, the first missionary to that section, who from this point made journeys in every direction to the Hudson's Bay Company's posts and Indian camps.

Following him, later on, the Roman Catholic Church sent in her missionaries. These, at the time of which I write, had a church in the Fort, and the beginning of a mission out north, about nine miles from the Fort; also one at Lake St. Ann's, some forty miles distant. When the Rev. Thomas Woolsey came into the North-West, he too made Edmonton his headquarters for some years, and, like his predecessor, travelled from camp to camp and from post to post.

Even in those early days, one could not help predicting a bright future for this important point, for in every direction from Edmonton, as a centre, Nature has been lavish with her gifts. The physical foundations of empire are here to be found in rich profusion, and in 1862, having gone into and come out of Edmonton by several different directions, I felt that I would run but little risk in venturing to prophesy that it would by-and-by become a great metropolis.

The second day of January, 1863, saw a considerable party of travellers wind out of the gate of the Fort and, descending the hill, take the ice and begin the race down the Big Saskatchewan; Mr. Chatelaine, of Fort Pitt, and Mr. Pambrun, of Lac-la-biche, with their men, making, with our party, a total of eight trains. There being no snow, we had to follow the windings of the river. For the first eighty or ninety miles our course was to be the same, and it was pleasant, in this land of isolation, to fall in with so many travelling companions.

It was late in the day when we got away, but both men and dogs were fresh, so we made good time and camped for the night some twenty-five miles from the Fort. Climbing the first bank, we pulled into a clump of spruce, and soon the waning light of day gave place to the bright glare of our large camp-fire. Frozen ground and a few spruce boughs were beneath us and the twinkling stars overhead.

There being at this time no snow, our home for the night is soon ready, the kettles boiled, the tea made and pemmican chopped loose, and though we are entirely without bread or fruit or vegetables, yet we drink our tea, gnaw our pemmican and enjoy ourselves. The twenty-five-mile run and the intense cold have made us very hungry. Most of our company are old pioneers, full of incident and story of life in the far north, or out on the " Big Plains " to the south. We feed our dogs, we tell our stories, we pile the long logs of wood on our big fire, and alternately change our position, back then front to the fire. We who have been running hard, and whose clothes are wet with perspiration, now become ourselves the clothes-horses whereon to dry these things before we attempt to sleep. Then we sing a hymn, have a word of prayer, and turn in.

The great fire burns down, the stars glitter through the crisp, frosty air, the aurora dances over our heads and flashes in brilliant colors about our camp, the trees and the ice crack with the intense cold, but we sleep on until between one and two, when we are again astir. Our huge fire once more flings its glare away out through the surrounding trees and into the cold night. A hot cup of tea, a small chunk of pemmican, a short prayer, and hitching up our dogs, tying up our sled loads and wrapping up our passengers, we are away once more on the ice of this great inland river. The yelp of a dog as the sharp whip touches him is answered from either forest-clad bank by numbers of coyotes and wolves; but regardless of these, "Marse!" is the word, and on we run, making fast time.

On our way up I had found a buck deer frozen into the ice, and had chopped the antlers from his head and "cached" them in a tree to take home with me; but when I told my new companions of my find, they were eager for the meat, which they said would be good. I had not yet eaten drowned meat, but when I came to think of it I saw there was reason in what they said, and so promised to do my best to find the spot where the buck was frozen in. As it was night—perhaps three o'clock—when we came to the place, I was a little dubious as to finding the deer. However, I was born with a large "bump of locality" and a good average memory, and presently we were chopping the drowned deer out of the ready-to-hand refrigerator. This done we drove on, and stopped for our second breakfast near the Vermilion. We were through and away from this before daylight, and hurrying on reached our turning-off point early in the afternoon, where we bade our friends good-bye, and, clambering up the north bank of the Saskatchewan, disappeared into the forest.

Taking our course straight for Smoking Lake, the whole length of which we travelled on the ice, we climbed the gently-sloping hill for two miles and were home again, having made the 120 miles in less than two days.

When I jumped out of bed next morning my feet felt as if I were foundered, because of the steady run on the frozen ground and harder ice; but this soon passed away. Mr. O. B., whom we had left at home, was greatly rejoiced at our return. He had been very lonely. I described to him our visit, and told him of the nice fat, tender beef on which the Chief Factor had regaled us on Christmas and New Year's day; and surely it was not my fault that, when the portion of the meat of the drowned deer which had been brought home was cooked, he thought it was Edmonton beef, and pronounced it "delicious," and partook largely of it, and later on was terribly put out to learn it was a bit of a drowned animal we had found in the river.

Holidays past, we faced our work, which was varied and large: fish to be hauled home; provisions to be sought for, and, when found, traded from the Indians; timber to be got out and hauled some distance; lumber to be "whipped,"—that is, cut by the whip-saw; freight to be hauled for Mr. Woolsey, who had some in store or as a loan at Whitefish Lake—all this gave us no time for loitering. Men, horses, dogs, all had to move. Moreover, we had to make our own dog and horse sleds, and sew the harness for both dogs and horses. That for the dogs we made out of tanned moose skins; that for the horses and oxen, out of partly tanned buffalo hide, known as "power flesh," the significance of which I could never comprehend, unless the sewing of them, which was powerfully tedious, was what was meant. Turn which way you would there was plenty to do, and, from the present day standpoint, very little to do it with.

Mr. Woolsey and Mr. O. B. kept down the shack, and the rest of us—that is, Williston, William, Neils and myself—went at the rest of the work. First we hauled the balance of our fish home, then we made a trip to Whitefish Lake and brought the freight which had been left there. Mr. Steinhauer and two of his daughters accompanied us back to Smoking Lake, the former to confer with his brother missionary, and the girls to become the pupils of Mr. Woolsey. The opportunity of being taught even the rudiments was exceedingly rare in those days in the North-West, and Mr. Steinhauer was only too glad to take the offer of his brother missionary to help in this way. The snow was now from a foot to twenty inches deep. The cold was keen. To make trails through dense forests and across trackless plains, to camp where night caught us, without tent or any other dwelling, and with only the blue sky above us and the crisp snow and frozen ground beneath, were now our every-day experience.

CHAPTER II.

A foraging expedition—Our hungry camp—A welcome feast—Dogs, sleds and buffalo bull in a tangle—In a Wood Cree encampment—Chief Child, Maskepetoon and Ka-kake—Indian hospitality—Incidents of the return trip.

ABOUT the middle of January we started for the plains to find the Indians, and, if possible, secure provisions and fresh meat from them. William and Neils, with horses and sleds, preceded us some days. Williston and I in the meantime went for the last load of fish, then we followed our men out to the great plains. In those days travelling with horses was tedious. You had to give the animals time to forage in the snow, or they would not stand the trip. From forty to sixty miles per day would be ordinary progress for dogs and drivers, but from ten to twenty would be enough for horses in the deep snow and cold of winter; thus it came to pass that, although William and Neils had preceded us some days, nevertheless we camped with them our second night out, close beside an old buffalo pound which had been built by the Indians.

It was said by the old Indians that if you took the wood of a pound for your camp-fire, a storm would be the result; and as we did take of the wood that night, a storm came sure enough, and William's horses were far away next morning. As we had but little provisions, Williston and I did not wait, but leaving the most of our little stock of dried meat with the horse party, we went on in the storm, and keeping at it all day, made a considerable distance in a south-easterly direction, where we hoped to fall in with Indians or buffaloes, or possibly a party bent on the same errand as ourselves from the sister mission at Whitefish Lake.

That night both men and dogs ate sparingly, for the simple reason that we did not have any more to eat. In these northern latitudes a night in January in the snow with plenty of food is, under the best of circumstances, a hardship; but when both tired men and faithful dogs are on "short commons" the gloom seems darker, the cold keener, the loneliness greater than usual. At any rate, that is how Williston and I felt the night I refer to. The problem was clear on the blackboard before us as we sat and vainly tried to think it out, for there was very little talking round our camp-fire that night. The known quantities were: an immense stretch of unfamiliar country before us; deep, loose snow everywhere around us; our food all gone; both of us in a large measure "tenderfeet." The unknown: Where were the friendly Indians and the buffaloes, and where was food to be found? But being tired and young we went to sleep, and with the morning star were waiting for the daylight in a more hopeful condition of mind.

Driving on in the drifting snow, about 10 a.m. we came upon a fresh track of dog-sleds going in our direction. This, then, must be the party from Whitefish Lake. The thought put new life both into us and our dogs. Closely watching the trail, which was being drifted over very fast by the loose snow, we hurried on, and soon came to where these people had camped the night before. Pushing on, we came up to them about the middle of the afternoon. They turned out to be Peter Erasmus and some Indians from Whitefish Lake Mission; but, alas for our hopes of food, like ourselves they were without provisions. However, we drove on as fast as we could, and had the supreme satisfaction of killing a buffalo cow just before sundown that same evening. Very soon the animal was butchered and on our sleds, and finding a suitable clump of timber, we camped for the night. Making a good large camp-fire, very soon we were roasting and boiling and eating buffalo meat, to the great content of our inner man. What a contrast our camp this night to that of the previous one! Then, hunger and loneliness and considerable anxiety; now, feasting and anecdote and joke and fun. Our dogs, also, were in better spirits.

There was one drawback—we had no salt. My companion Williston had left what little we had in one of our camps. He pretended he did not care for salt, and he and the others laughed at me because I longed for it so much. The fresh meat was good, but "Oh, if I only had some salt!" was an oft-repeated expression from my lips. Later we fell in with old Ben Sinclair, who sympathized with me very much, and rummaging in the dirty, grimy sack in which he carried his tobacco and moccasins and mending material, he at last brought up a tiny bit of salt tied up in the corner of a small rag, saying: "My wife Magened, he very good woman, he put that there; you may have it;" and thankful I was for the few grains of salt. As Williston had lost ours, and had laughed at me for mourning over the loss, and especially as the few grains old Ben gave me would not admit of it, I did not offer him a share, but made my little portion last for the rest of that journey.

Six hungry, hard-travelled men and twenty-four hungrier and also harder-travelled dogs

"The dogs and sleds went sliding in around him." (*Page 23.*)

left very little of that buffalo cow (though a big and fat animal) to carry out of the camp. Supper, or several suppers, for six men and twenty-four dogs, and then breakfast for six men, and the cow was about gone; but now we had pretty good hope of finding more. This we did as we journeyed on, and at the end of two days' travel we sighted the smoke of a large camp of Indians.

Nothing special had happened during those two days, except that once our dogs and an old buffalo bull got badly tangled up, and we had to kill the bull to unravel the tangle. It happened in this wise: We started the bull, and he galloped off, almost on our course, so we let our dogs run after him, and the huge, clumsy fellow took straight across a frozen lake, and coming upon some glare ice just as the dogs came up to him, he slipped and fell, and the dogs and sleds went sliding in all around him. Thus the six trains got tangled up all around the old fellow, who snorted and shook his head, and kicked, but could not get up. We had to kill him to release our dogs and sleds.

The camp we came to had about two hundred lodges, mostly Wood Crees. They were glad to see us, and welcomed us right hospitably. We went into Chief Child's tent, and made our home there for the short time we were in the camp; but we may be said to have boarded all over this temporary village, for I think I must have had a dozen suppers in as many different tents the first evening of our arrival; and I could not by any means accept all the invitations I had showered upon me. While eating a titbit of buffalo in one tent, and giving all the items of news from the north I knew, and asking and answering questions, behold! another messenger would come in, and tell me he had been sent to take me to another big man's lodge —and thus, until midnight, I went from tent to tent, sampling the culinary art of my Indian friends, and imparting and receiving information. I had a long chat with the grand old chief, Maskepetoon; renewed my acquaintance with the sharp-eyed and wiry hunter and warrior, Ka-kake, and made friends with a bright, fine-looking young man who had recently come from a war expedition. He had been shot right through his body, just missing the spine, and was now convalescing. My new friend, some four or five years after our first meeting, gave up tribal war and paganism, and heartily embraced Christianity. He became as the right hand of the missionary, and to-day is head man at Saddle Lake.

Without recognizing the fact, I was now fairly in the field as a pioneer, and taking my first lessons in the university of God as a student in a great new land. Running after a dog-train all day, partaking of many suppers, talking more or less all the time until midnight, then to bed—thus the first night was spent in camp.

Next morning we traded our loads of provisions—calfskin bags of pounded meat, cakes of hard tallow, bladders of marrow-fat, bales of dried meat, and buffalo tongues. In a short time Williston and I had all we could pack on our sleds, or at any rate all our dogs could haul home. And now it required some skill and planning to load our sleds. To pack and wrap and lash securely as a permanent load for home, some four hundred pounds of tongues and cakes and bladders of grease and bags of pounded meat, on a small toboggan, some eight feet by one foot in size; then on the top of this to tie our own and our dogs' provisions for the return journey, also axe, and kettle, and change of duffels and moccasins; and in the meantime answer a thousand questions that men and women and children who, as they looked on or helped, kept plying us with, took some time and patient work; but by evening we were ready to make an early start next day.

In the meantime the hunters had been away killing and bringing in meat and robes. With the opening light, and all day long, the women had been busy scraping hides and dressing robes and leather, pounding meat, rendering tallow, chopping bones wherewith to make what was termed "marrow-fat," bringing in wood, besides sewing garments and making and mending moccasins. Only the men who had just come home from a war party, or those who came in the day before with a lot of meat and a number of hides, were now the loungers, resting from the heavy fatigues of the chase or war. The whole scene was a study of life under new phases, and as I worked and talked I was taking it all in and adapting language and idiom and thought to my new surroundings.

Another long evening of many invitations and many suppers, also of continuous catechism and questionings, then a few hours' sleep, during which the temperature has become fearfully cold, and with early morn we are catching our dogs, who are now rested, and with what food we gave them and that which they have stolen have perceptibly fattened.

Our Whitefish Lake friends are ready also, and we make a start. Our loads are high and heavy. Many an upset takes place. To right the load, to hold it back going down hill, to push up the steep hills, to run and walk all the time, to take our turn in breaking the trail (for we are going as straight as possible for home, and will not strike our out-bound trail for many miles, then only to find it drifted over)—all this soon takes the romance out of winter tripping with dogs; but we plod on and camp some thirty-five or forty miles from the Indian camp. The already tired drivers must work hard at making camp and cutting and packing wood before this day's work is done; then supper and rest, and prayer and bed, and long before daylight next morning we are away, and by pushing on make from forty to fifty miles our second day.

That night we sent a message back to the Indian camp. The message was about buffaloes, of which we had seen quite a number of herds that afternoon. The messenger was a dog. Peter Erasmus had bought a very fine-looking dog from an old woman, and I incidentally heard her, as she was catching the dog, say to him: "This is now the sixth time I have sold you, and you came home five times. I expect you will do so again." And sure enough the big fine-looking fellow turned out a fraud. Peter was tired of him, and was about to let him go, when I suggested using him to tell the Indians about the buffaloes we had seen; so a message in syllabics was written and fastened to the dog's neck, and he was let loose. He very soon left our camp, and, as I found out later, was in the Indian camp when the people began to stir next morning. We let him go about eight o'clock at night, and before daylight next morning he had made the two days' journey traversed by us. As an Indian would say, "The old woman's medicine is strong!"

There were six very weary men in our camp that night, thirty-three years ago. Floundering through the snow for two long days, pushing and righting and holding back those heavy sleds, whipping up lazy dogs, etc., chopping and carrying wood, shovelling snow—well, we wanted our supper. But after supper, what a change! Joke and repartee, incident and story followed, and while the wolves howled and the wind whistled and the cold intensified, with our big blazing fire we were, in measure, happy. Three of the six have been dead many years; the other three, though aging fast, are now and then camping as of old, still vigorous and hale.

During the next morning's tramp we separated, each party taking the direct course for home. That afternoon we met William and Neils, who had been all this time finding their horses, which strayed away the night of the storm, when we camped together by the old pound. Surely the spirit of the old structure had been avenged because of our burning some of it, for the storm had come, the horses had been lost, and our men had been in a condition of semi-starvation for some days. We told them where they could find buffaloes and the Indian camp, gave them some provisions and drove on. Having the track, we made the old pound the same evening, and, nothing daunted, proceeded to make firewood of its walls. To our camp there came that night the tall young Indian Pakan, who is now the chief of the Whitefish and Saddle Lake Reserves. He seemed to resent the desecration of the pound, but our supper and company and the news of buffaloes made him forget this for the time. He and two or three others were camped not far off, on their way out to the plains.

Two long days more, with the road very heavy, and sometimes almost no road at all, brought us late the second night to our shack, where Mr. Woolsey and Mr. O. B. were delighted to greet us once more. They had been lonely and were anxious about us.

CHAPTER III.

Scarcity of food—The winter packet—Start for Edmonton for the eastern mails—A lonely journey—Arrive at Fort Edmonton—Start for home—Camping in a storm—Improvising a "Berlin"—Old Draffan—Sleeping on a dog-sled *en route*—A hearty welcome home.

THAT trip with dog-train was enough for Williston. He did not want any more of such work, so I took an Indian boy who had joined our party and started out again. Later on I traded Williston to William for Neils, the Norwegian, who made several trips with me. During that winter the Indian camps at which we could obtain provisions were never nearer than about 150 miles, and were sometimes much farther away; and as we intended building the next spring on the site of the new mission, at the river, we had to make every effort to secure a sufficiency of provisions. When we had neither flour nor vegetables, animal food alone went fast. Then, besides the hauling of food long distances, we had to transport lumber and timber and other material from where we were living to the new and permanent site on the river bank, which was some thirty-five miles distant. Sometimes with the dog-teams we took down a load of lumber to the river and returned the same day, thus making the seventy-mile round trip in the day. The horses would take from three to four days for the same trip.

It was some time in February that, having started from our first encampment on the way out, long before daylight one dark morning we saw the glimmer of a camp-fire, and wondered who it could be; but as the light was right on our road, we found when we came up that it was the one winter packet from the east on its way to Edmonton. Mr. Hardisty was in charge of the party, and the reason they had stopped and made a fire on our road—which they should have crossed at right angles—was that through the darkness of the winter morning they had missed their way, and were waiting for daylight to show them their course.

Mr. Hardisty gave me some items of news from the outside world, and also told me, what was tantalizing in the extreme, that there were letters for Mr. Woolsey and myself in the packet, but that this was sealed and could not be opened until they reached Edmonton. How I did long for those letters from home and the loved ones there. But longing would not open the sealed packet box.

With the first glimmering of day we parted, the winter packet to continue its way through the deep snow and uncertain trail on to Edmonton; we to make our way out to the Indian camps. These were continually moving with the buffalo, so that the place that knew them to-day might possibly never know them again forever, so big is this vast country, and so migratory in their habits are its peoples.

In due time we found one of the camps, and trading our loads made for home; but as this was the stormy and windy season of the year, we made slow progress. Finally we reached Mr. Woolsey, and I importuned him to let me go for our mail, which he finally consented to do, but said he could not spare anyone to go with me. However, I was so eager that I resolved to go alone. My plan was to send Neils and the boy Ephraim out for more provisions, and I would accompany them as far as the spot where we had seen the packet men some two weeks before. Then I should take their trail, and try and keep it to Edmonton. Mr. Woolsey very reluctantly assented to all this.

About three o'clock one dark, cloudy morning found us at the "parting of the ways," and bidding Neils and Ephraim good-bye, I put on my snowshoes and took the now more or less covered trail of the packet men. I had about 250 pounds of a load, consisting of ammunition and tobacco that Mr. Woolsey had borrowed from the Hudson's Bay Company, and was now returning by me. I had great faith in my lead dog "Draffan," a fine big black fellow, whose sleek coat had given him his name, "Fine-cloth." In fact, all four of my dogs were noble fellows, and away we went, Draffan smelling and feeling out the very indistinct trail, and I running behind on snowshoes. It was my first trip alone, and I could not repress a feeling of isolation; but then the object, "letters from home," was constantly in my thoughts and spurring me on. By daylight I came to the snow-drifted dinner camp of the packet men; by half-past ten I was at their night encampment. I am doing well, thought I, and here I unharnessed my dogs and made a fire, and by melting snow boiled my kettle, but did not feel very much like eating or drinking. The whole thing was inexpressibly lonely. The experience was a new one and not too pleasant.

My dogs hardly had time to roll and shake themselves from the long run of the morning when I was sticking their heads into the collars again, and away jumped the faithful brutes, Draffan scenting and feeling the much-blinded road. On we went, the dogs with their load, and I on my light snowshoes, keeping up a smart run across plains, through bluffs of willow and poplar, over hills and along valleys. About the middle of the afternoon, or later, I noticed the snow was lessening, and presently I took off my snowshoes, and also my coat, and tying these on the sled, started up the dogs with a sudden sharp command, and away they jumped. We increased our speed, and went flying westward toward the setting sun; for though I had never been over this country before, I had an idea that Edmonton was about on our course. On towards sundown I noticed a well-timbered range of dark hills in the distance, and said to myself, "There is where we must camp," and I could not help already feeling a premonition of great loneliness coming over me.

On we sped, the dogs at a sharp trot, with an occasional run, and I on what you might call two-thirds or three-fourths speed, when all of a sudden we came into a well-beaten road, which converged into our trail, and now, with the solid, smooth track under their feet, my noble team fairly raced away, making my sledge swing in good shape.

Thinking to myself that I might catch up to or meet some party travelling in this evidently well-frequented road, I put on my coat, seated myself on the sled, and my hardy team went flying on the best tracked road they had struck that winter. Presently we came to the edge of a great hill, which I found to be but the beginning of a large, deep valley. Hardly had I time to get astride the sled, and with my feet brake or help to steer its course, when down, down, down, at a dead hard run, went my dogs. Then over a sloping bottom, and to my great astonishment out we came on the banks of a big river.

"What is this?" thought I; "surely I have missed my way." I had never heard of a large stream emptying into the Saskatchewan from the south side. While thus perplexed and anxious, my dogs took a short jump over a cut bank, and I was landed, sled and dogs and all, on the ice of this big river. Then I looked up westward, and to my surprise saw in the waning light the wings or fans of the old wind-mill which stood on the hill back of Fort Edmonton. I could hardly believe my eyes, but on sped my eager dogs. Soon we were climbing the opposite bank, and presently, just as the guard was about to shut the eastern gate of the Fort, we dashed in and were at our journey's end.

"Where did you come from to-day, John?" asked my friend, Mr. Hardisty. My reply was, "About fifteen miles north of where we saw you the other morning." "No," said he; but nevertheless it was true. They had travelled all that day after we had seen them, as they left us at the first approach of daylight; then they had started long before daylight the next morning, and it was evening when they reached Edmonton; while I had done the same distance and fifteen miles more—that is, I had made a good round hundred miles that day, my first trip alone.

Right glad I was at being thus relieved from camping alone that night, and with my letters all cheering, and the kind friends of the place, I thoroughly enjoyed the hospitality of Old Fort Edmonton. It was Friday night when I reached the Fort. Spending Saturday and Sunday with the Hudson's Bay officers and men, I started on my return trip Monday, about 10.30 a.m., and by night had made the camp where I had lunched on the way out. To some extent I had got over the shrinking from being alone, so I chopped and carried wood for my camp, made myself as comfortable as I could, fed my dogs, and listened to the chorus of wolves and coyotes as they howled dismally around me. Then the wind got up, and with gusts of wild fury came whistling through the trees which composed the little bluff in which I was camped. Soon it began to drift, so I turned up my sled on its edge to the windward, and stretching my feet to the fire, wrapped myself in buffalo and blanket, and went to sleep.

When I awoke I jumped up and made a fire,

and looking at my watch, saw it was two o'clock. The wind had become a storm. I went out of the woods to where I thought the trail should be, and felt for it with my feet (for I had grown to have great faith in Draffan and his wonderful instinct, and thought that if I could start him right he would be likely to keep right), and there under the newly drifted snow was the frozen track. I then went back to the camp and harnessed my dogs, and as I had little or no load, I made an improvised cariole, or what was termed a "Berlin," out of my wrapper and sled lashings, and when ready drove out to where I had discovered the track.

The storm was now raging, the night was wild, and the cold intense; but, wrapped in my warm robe, I stretched myself in the "Berlin," and getting as flat as possible in order to lessen the chances of upsetting, when ready I gave the word to Draffan, saw that he took the right direction, and then covering up went to sleep. With sublime faith in that dog I slept on. If I woke up for a moment, I merely listened for the jingle of my dog-bells, and by the sound satisfied myself that my team were travelling steadily, and then went to sleep again.

When coming up I had noticed a long side hill, and I said to myself: "If we are on the right track I will most assuredly upset at that point"—and sure enough I did wake up to find myself rolling, robe and all, down the slope of the hill. I was compensated for the discomfort by being thus assured that my faithful dogs had kept the right track. Jumping up, I shook myself and the robe, righted the sled, stretched the robe into it, and then giving my leader a caress and a word of encouragement, I put on my snowshoes and away we went at a good run, old Draffan picking the way with unerring instinct. Thus we kept it up until daylight, when we stopped and I unharnessed the dogs, and, making a fire, boiled my kettle and had breakfast. Then, starting once more, I determined to cut across some of the points of the square we had made coming up; and for about four hours we went straight across country, and striking our provision trail opposite Egg Lake, I took off my snowshoes and got into the "Berlin." My dogs bounded away on the home-stretch, we still having about forty or forty-five miles to go, and it was already past noon.

All day it had stormed, but now we were on familiar ground, and right merrily my noble dogs rang the bells, as across bits of prairie and through thickening woods we took our way northward. I was so elated at having successfully made the trip up to this point, that

I could not sit still very long, but, running and riding, kept on, never stopping for lunch. Thus the early dusk of the stormy day found us at the southerly end of Smoking Lake, and some twelve or fifteen miles from home. Here I again wrapped myself in my robe, and lying flat in the sled, felt I could very safely leave the rest to old Draffan and a kind Providence, and go to sleep, which I did, to wake up as the dogs were climbing the steep little bank at the north end of the lake. Then a run of two miles and I was home again.

Mr. Woolsey was so overjoyed he took me in his arms, and almost wept over me. He brought dogs, sled and my whole outfit into the house. The kind-hearted old man had passed a period of great anxiety; had been sorry a thousand times that he had consented to my going to Edmonton; had dreamed of my being lost, of my bleeding to death, of my freezing stiff; but now with the first tinkle of my dog-bells he was out peering into the darkness, and shouting, "Is that you, John?" and my answer, he assured me, filled him with joy. He did not ask for his mail, did not think of it for a long time, he was so thankful that the boy left in his care had come back to him safe and sound. For my part I was glad to be home again. The uncertain road, the long distance, the deep snow, the continuous drifting storm, the awful loneliness, were all past. I had found Edmonton, had brought the mail, was home again beside our own cheery fire, and was a proud and happy boy.

In a day or two Neils and Ephraim came in from the camp, and we once more, a reunited party, made another start for more provisions, and, later on, yet another for the same purpose, never finding the Indians in the same place, but always following them up. We were successful in reaching their camps and in securing our loads; so that my first winter on the Saskatchewan gave me the opportunity of covering a large portion of the country, and becoming acquainted with a goodly number of the Indian people. I also had constant practice in the language, and was now quite familiar with it.

CHAPTER IV.

Trip to Whitefish Lake—Mr. Woolsey as a dog-driver—Rolling down a side hill—Another trip to Edmonton—Mr. O. B. as a passenger—Perils of travel by ice—Narrow escape of Mr. O. B.—A fraud exposed—Profanity punished—Arrival at Edmonton—Milton and Cheadle—Return to Victoria.

SOME time in March, Mr. Woolsey, wishing to confer with his brother missionary, Mr. Steinhauer, concluded to go to Whitefish Lake, and to take the Steinhauer girls home at the same time. He, moreover, determined to take the train of dogs Neils had been driving, and drive himself; but as there had been no direct traffic from where we were to Whitefish Lake, and as the snow was yet quite deep, we planned to take our provision trail out south until we would come near to the point where our road converged with one which came from Whitefish Lake to the plains. This meant travelling more than twice the distance for the sake of a good road, but even this paid us when compared with making a new road through a forest country in the month of March, when the snow was deep.

We were about two and a half days making the trip, travelling about 130 miles, but, burdened as Ephraim and I were with three passengers, "the longest way round proved the shortest way home."

Mr. Woolsey was not a good dog-driver. He could not run, or even walk at any quick pace, so he had to sit wedged into his cariole, from start to finish, between camps, while I kept his train on the road ahead of mine; for if he upset—which he often did—he could not right himself, and I had to run ahead and fix him up. His dogs very soon got to know that their driver was a fixture on the sled, and also that I was away behind the next train and could not very well get at them because of the narrow road, and the great depth of snow on either side of it. However, things reached a climax when we were passing through a hilly, rolling country on the third morning of our trip. Those dogs would not even run down hill fast enough to keep the sleigh on its bottom, and I had to run forward and right Mr. Woolsey and his cariole a number of times. Presently, coming to a side hill, Mr. Woolsey, in his sled, rolled over and over, like a log, to the foot of the slope.

There, fast in the cariole, and wedged in the snow, lay the missionary. The lazy dogs had gently accommodated themselves to the rolling of the sled, and also lay at the foot of the hill, seemingly quite content to rest for awhile.

Now, thought I, is my chance, and without touching Mr. Woolsey or his sled, I went at those dogs, and in a very short time put the fear of death into them, so that when I spoke to them afterwards they jumped. Then I unravelled them and straightened them out, and rescuing Mr. Woolsey from his uncomfortable position, I spoke the word, and the very much quickened dogs sprang into their collars as if they meant it, and after this we made better time.

Mr. and Mrs. Steinhauer were delighted to have their daughters home, and also glad to have a visit from our party. We spent two very pleasant days with these worthy people, who were missionaries of the true type. Going back I hitched my own dogs to Mr. Woolsey's cariole, and thus kept him right side up with much less trouble, and also made better time back to Smoking Lake.

With the approach of spring we prepared to move down to the river. We put up a couple of stagings, also a couple of buffalo-skin lodges, in one of which Mr. Woolsey and Mr. O. B. took up their abode, while the rest of our party kept on the road, bringing down from the old place our goods and chattels, lumber and timber, etc. As the days grew warmer, we who were handling dogs had to travel most of the time in the night, as then the snow and track were frozen. While the snow lasted we slept and rested during the warm hours of the day, and in the cool of the morning and evening, and all night long, we kept at work transporting our materials to the site of the new mission. The last of the season is a hard time for the dog-driver. The night-work, the glare or reflection of the snow, both by sun and moonlight; the subsidence of the snow on either side of the road, causing constant upsetting of sleds; the melting of the snow, making your feet wet and sloppy almost all the time; then the pulling, and pushing, and lifting, and walking, and running,—these were the inevitable experiences. Indeed, one had to be tough and hardy and willing, or he would never succeed as a traveller and tripper in the "great lone land" in those days.

The snow had almost disappeared, and the first geese and ducks were beginning to arrive, when suddenly one evening Mr. Steinhauer and Peter Erasmus turned up, *en route* to Edmonton; and Mr. Woolsey took me to one side and said, "John, I am about tired of Mr. O. B. Could you not take him to Edmonton and leave him there. You might join this party now going there."

In a very few hours I was ready, and the

same night we started on the ice, intending to keep the river to Edmonton. The night was clear and cold, and for some time the travelling was good; but near daylight, when about thirty miles on our way, we met an overflow flood coming down on top of the ice. There must have been from sixteen to eighteen inches of water, creating quite a current, and as we were on the wrong side of the river it behoved us to cross as soon as possible, and go into camp. There was a thick scum of sharp float ice on the top of the flood, about half an inch thick. When I drove my dogs into the overflow they had almost to swim, and the cariole, notwithstanding I was steadying it, would float and wobble in the current. Unfortunately, as the cold water began to soak into the sled, and reached my passenger, Mr. O. B., he blamed me for it, and presently began to curse me roundly, declaring I was doing it on purpose. All this time I was wading in the water and keeping the sled from upsetting; but when he continued his profanity I couldn't stand it any longer, so just dumped him right out into the overflow and went on. However, when I looked back and saw the old fellow staggering through the water, and fending his legs with his cane from the sharp ice, I returned and helped him ashore, but told him I would not stand any more swearing.

We then climbed the bank on the north side, and had to remain there for two days till the waters subsided. About eight o'clock the second night the ice was nearly dry, and frozen sufficiently for us to make a fresh start. We proceeded up the river, picking our way with great care, for there were now many holes in the ice, caused by the swift currents which had been above as well as beneath for the last two days. My passenger never slept, but sat there watching those holes, and dreading to pass near them, constantly afraid of drowning—in fact, I never travelled with anyone so much in dread of death as he was.

Morning found us away above Sturgeon River, and as the indications pointed to a speedy "break up," we determined to push on. Presently we came to a place where the banks were steep and the river open on either side. The ice, though still intact in the middle, was submerged by a volume of water running nearly crossways in the river. Some of our party began to talk of turning back, but as we were now within twenty-five miles of Edmonton, I was loath to return with my old passenger, so concluded to risk the submerged ice-bridge before us. I told Mr. O. B. to get out of the cariole; then I fastened two lines to the sled, took hold of one myself, and gave him the other, telling him to hang on for dear life if he should break through. I then drove my dogs in. Away they went across, we following at the end of the lines, stepping as lightly as we could, and as the dogs got out on the strong ice they pulled us after them.

Having crossed, I set to work to wring out the blankets and robes in the cariole, Mr. O. B. looking on. At the bottom there was a parchment robe—that is, an undressed hide. This, I said, I would not take any further, as it was comparatively useless anyway, but now, soaked and heavy, it was an actual encumbrance.

"You will take it along," said Mr. O. B.

"No, I will not," said I; but as there was good ice as far as I could see ahead, I told him to go on, and that I would overtake him as soon as I was through fixing the things in the sled. Reluctantly he started, and by-and-by when I came to the hide I found it so heavy that I did as I said I would, and pitched it into the stream. When I came up with Mr. O. B., instead of stepping into the cariole, he turned up everything to look for the hide, and, not finding it, began to rave at me, using the foulest and most blasphemous language.

I merely looked at him and said, "Get in, or I will leave you here." He saw I was in earnest, and got into the sled in no good humor, and on we drove; but as I ran behind I was planning some punishment for the old sinner, who had posed as such a saint while with Mr. Woolsey.

Very soon everything came as if ready to hand for my purpose. As we were skirting the bank we came to a place where the ice sloped to the current, and just there the water was both deep and rapid. Here I took a firm grip of the lines from the back of the cariole, and watching for the best place, shouted to the dogs to increase their speed. Then I gave a stern, quick "Chuh!" which made the leader jump close to the edge of the current, and as the sled went swinging down the sloping ice, I again shouted "Whoa!" and down in their tracks dropped my dogs. Out into the current, over the edge of the ice, slid the rear end of the cariole. Mr. O. B. saw he dare not jump out, for the ice would have broken, and he would have gone under into the strong current. There he sat, his eyes bulging out with fear as he cried, "For God's sake, John, what are you going to do?" while I stood holding the line, which, if I slackened, would let him into the rapid water, from which there seemed to be no earthly means of rescue.

After a while I said, "Well, Mr. O. B., are you ready now to apologize for, and take back the foul language you, without reason, heaped on

"There he sat, his eyes bulging out with fear." (*Page 48.*)

me a little while since?" And Mr. O. B., in most abject tones and terms, did make ample apology. Then slackening the line a little, I let the sled flop up and down in the current, and finally accepted his apology on condition that he would behave himself in the future. My dogs quickly pulled him out of his peril, and on we went. Presently we were joined by Mr. Steinhauer and Peter, who had gone across a point, they having light sleds, which enabled them to make their way for a short distance on the bare ground.

We reached Edmonton that evening, and I was glad to transfer my charge to some one else's care. I was not particular who took him, for, like Mr. Woolsey, I was tired of the old fraud.

The Chief Factor said to me that evening, "So you brought Mr. O. B. to Edmonton. You will have to pay ten shillings for every day he remains in the Fort."

"Excuse me, sir," I answered, "I brought him to the foot of the hill, down at the landing, and left him there. If he comes into the Fort I am not responsible."

Shortly after this Lord Milton and Dr. Cheadle came along *en route* across the mountains, and Mr. O. B. joined their party. If any one should desire more of his history, these gentlemen wrote a book descriptive of their journey, and in this our hero appears. I am done with him, for the present at any rate.

Spring was now open, the snow nearly gone, and we had to make our way back from Edmonton as best we could. I cached the cariole, hired a horse, packed him with my dog harness, blankets, and food, and thus reached Victoria, which father had designated as the name of the new mission. My dogs, having worked faithfully for many months, and having travelled some thousands of miles, sometimes under most trying circumstances, were now entering upon their summer vacation. How they gambolled and ran and hunted as they journeyed homeward!

CHAPTER V.

Mr. Woolsey's ministrations—An exciting foot-race—Building operations—Gardening—Stolen (?) buffalo tongues—Addled duck eggs as a relish—A lesson in cooking—A lucky shot—Precautions against hostile Indians.

WITH the opening spring Indians began to come in from the plains, and for several weeks we had hundreds of lodges beside us. Mr. Woolsey was kept busy holding meetings, attending councils, visiting the sick, acting as doctor and surgeon, magistrate and judge; for who else had these people to come to but the missionary? A number of them had accepted Christianity, but the majority were still pagan, and these were full of curiosity as to the missionary and his work, and keenly watching every move of the "praying man" and his party. The preacher may preach ever so good, but he himself is to these people the exponent of what he preaches, and they judge the Gospel he presents by himself. If he fails to measure up in manliness and liberality and general manhood, then they think there is no more use in listening to his teaching. Very early in my experience it was borne in upon me that the missionary, to obtain influence on the people, must be fitted to lead in all matters. If short of this, their estimate of him would be low, and their respect proportionately small, and thus his work would be sadly handicapped all through.

While Mr. Woolsey was constantly at work among the people, the rest of us were fencing and planting a field, whipsawing lumber, taking out timber up the river, and rafting it down to the mission, also building a house, and in many ways giving object lessons of industry and settled life to this nomadic and restless people.

It was at this time that I got a name for myself by winning a race. The Indians had challenged two white men to run against two of their people. The race was to be run from Mr. Woolsey's tent to and around another tent that stood out on the plain, and back home again—a distance in all of rather more than two-thirds of a mile. I was asked to be one of the champions of the white men, and a man by the name of McLean was selected as the other. Men, women, and children in crowds came to see the race, and Mr. Woolsey seemed as interested as any. The two Indians came forth gorgeous in breech-cloth and paint. My partner lightened his costume, but I ran as I worked.

At a signal we were away, and with ease I was soon ahead. When I turned the tent, I saw that the race was ours, for my partner was the first man to meet me, and he was a long distance ahead of the Indians. When within three hundred yards of the goal, a crack runner sprang out from before me. He had been lying in the grass, with his dressed buffalo-skin over him, and springing up he let the skin fall from his naked body, then sped away, with the intention of measuring his speed with mine. I had my race already won, and needed not to run this fellow, but his saucy action nettled me to chase him, and I soon came up and passed him easily, coming in about fifty yards ahead.

Thus I had gained two races, testing both wind and speed. That race opened my way to many a lodge, and to the heart of many a friend in subsequent years. It was the best introduction I could have had to those hundreds of aborigines, among whom I was to live and work for years.

A few weeks sufficed to consume all the provisions the Indians had brought with them, and a very large part of ours also; so the tents were furled, and the people recrossed the Saskatchewan, and, ascending the steep hill, disappeared from our view for another period, during which they would seek the buffalo away out on the plains.

We went on with our work of planting this centre of Christian civilization. Though we had visits from small bands, coming and going all summer, the larger camps did not return until the autumn. All this time we were living in skin lodges. Mr. Woolsey aimed at putting up a large house, in the old-fashioned Hudson's Bay style—a frame of timber, with grooved posts in which tenoned logs were fitted into ten-foot spans—and as all the work of sawing and planing had to be done by hand, the progress was slow. My idea was to face long timber, and put up a solid blockhouse, which could be done so much more easily and quickly, and would be stronger in the end; but I was overruled, so we went on more slowly with the big house, and were smoked and sweltered in the tents all summer. However, taking out timber and rafting it down the river took up a lot of my time.

Then there was our garden to weed and hoe. One day when I was at this, we dined on buffalo tongue. Quite a number of these had been boiled to be eaten cold, and as our sleigh dogs were always foraging, it was necessary to put all food up on the stagings, or else the dogs would take it. As soon as I was through dinner I went back to my hoeing and weeding, but looking over at the tent, I saw Mr. Woolsey leaving it, and thought he must have forgotten to put those tongues away. As our variety was not great, I did not want the dogs to have these, so I ran over to the tent just in time to save them. I thought it would be well to make Mr. Woolsey more careful in the future; so, putting away the tongues, I scattered the dishes around the tent, and left things generally upset, as if a dozen dogs had been there, and then went back to my work, keeping a sharp watch on the tent.

When Mr. Woolsey came back he went into the tent, and very soon came out again shaking his fist at the dogs. Presently he shouted to me, "John, the miserable dogs have stolen all our tongues!"

"That is too bad," said I; "did you not put them away?"

"No, I neglected to," he answered. "I shall thrash every one of these thieving dogs."

Of course I did not expect him to do this, but at any rate I did not want to see him touch Draffan, my old leader, so I ran over to the tent, and could not help but laugh when I saw Mr. Woolsey catch one of the dogs, and, turning to me, say, "This old Pembina was actually licking his lips when I came back to the tent. I all but caught him in the act of stealing the tongues."

I can see old Pembina as he stood there

looking very sheepish and guilty. Mr. Woolsey stood with one hand grasping the string, and with the other uplifted, holding in it a small riding whip; but just as he was about to bring it down, the expected relenting came, and he said, as he untied the dog, "Poor fellow, it was my fault, anyway." I let him worry over the thought that the tongues were gone until evening, when I brought them out, and Mr. Woolsey, being an Englishman, was glad they were saved for future use.

Our principal food that summer was pemmican, or dried meat. We had neither flour nor vegetables, but sometimes, for a change, lived on ducks, and again varied our diet with duck eggs. We would boil the large stock ducks whole, and each person would take one, so that the individual occupying the head of the table was put to no trouble in carving. Each man in his own style did his own carving, and picked the bones clean at that. Then, another time, we would sit down to boiled duck eggs, many a dozen of these before us, and in all stages of incubation. While the older hands seemed to relish these, it took some time for me to learn that an egg slightly addled is very much improved in taste.

Our horses often gave us a lot of trouble, because of the extent of their range, and many a long ride I had looking them up. On one of these expeditions I was accompanied by an Indian boy, and, having struck the track, we kept on through the thickets and around lakes and swamps, till, after a while, we became very hungry. As we had no gun with us, the question arose, how were we to procure anything for food? My boy suggested hunting for eggs. I replied, "We cannot eat them raw." "We will cook them," he answered. So we unsaddled and haltered our horses, and, stripping off our clothes, waded out into the rushes and grasses of the little lake we were then beside. We soon found some eggs, and while I made the fire, my companion proceeded with what, to me, was a new mode of cooking eggs. He took the bark off a young poplar, and of this made a long tube, tying or hooping it with willow-bark; then he stopped up one end with mud from the lake shore, and, as the hollow of the tube was about the diameter of the largest egg we had, he very soon had it full of eggs. Stopping up the other end also with mud, he moved the embers from the centre of the fire, laid the tube in the hot earth, covered it over with ashes and coals, and in a few minutes we had a deliciously-cooked lunch of wild duck eggs. I had learned another lesson in culinary science.

On another horse-hunt we found the track

late in the day, and, following it up, saw that we must either go back to the mission for the night, or camp without provisions or blankets. The latter we could stand, as it was summer, but the former was harder to bear. While we were discussing what to do, we heard the calling of sand-hill cranes, and presently saw five flying at a distance from us. Watching them, we saw them light on the point of a hill about half a mile off. Laughingly, I said to my boy in Indian phraseology, "I will make sacrifice of a ball." So I got my gun-worm, drew the shot from my old flintlock gun, and dropped a ball in its place; and as there was no chance of a nearer approach to the cranes, I sighted one from where I stood, then elevated my gun, and fired. As we watched, we saw the bird fall over, and my boy jumped on his horse and went for our game. We then continued on the track as long as we could see it, and, as night drew on, pitched our camp beside some water, and made the crane serve us for both supper and breakfast. I might try a shot under the same conditions a hundred times more, and miss every time, but that one lucky hit secured to us a timely repast, and enabled us to continue on the trail of our horses, which we found about noon the next day.

We had to have lumber to make anything

like a home for semi-civilized men and women to dwell in. In my humble judgment, the hardest labor of a physical kind one could engage in is dog-driving, and the next to that "whip-sawing" lumber. I have had to engage in all manner of work necessary to the establishing of a settlement in new countries, but found nothing harder than these. I had plenty of the former last winter, and now occasionally try the latter, and, in the hot days of summer, find it desperately hard work.

In the midst of our building and manufacture of timber and lumber, rafting and hauling, fencing and planting, weeding and hoeing, every little while there would come in from the plains rumors of horse-stealing and scalp-taking. The southern Indians were coming north, and the northern Indians going south; and although we did not expect an attack, owing to our being so far north, and also because the Indian camps were between us and our enemies, nevertheless we felt it prudent to keep a sharp lookout, and conceal our horses as much as possible by keeping them some distance from where we lived. All this caused considerable riding and work and worry, and thus we were kept busy late and early.

CHAPTER VI.

The summer brigade—With the brigade down the Saskatchewan—A glorious panorama—Meet with father and mother on the way to Victoria—Privations of travel—A buffalo crossing—Arrival at Victoria—A church building begun—Peter Erasmus as interpreter.

ALONG about the latter part of July, the "Summer Brigade," made up of several inland boats left at Edmonton, and manned by men who had been on the plains for the first or summer trip for provisions and freight, now returned, passing us on its way to Fort Carlton to meet the regular brigades from Norway House and York Factory, as also the overland transport from Fort Garry, which came by ox carts. Mr. Hardisty was with the boats, and he invited me to join him until he should meet the brigade in which my father and mother had taken passage from Norway House. Mr. Woolsey kindly consented, so I gladly took this opportunity of going down to meet my parents and friends.

I had come up the Saskatchewan as far as Fort Carlton, and had gone three times on the ice up and down from Victoria to Edmonton; but this run down the river was entirely new to me and full of interest. The boats were fully manned, and the river was almost at flood-tide, so we made very quick time. Seven or eight big oars in the hands of those hardy voyageurs, keeping at it from early morning until late evening, with very little cessation, backed as they were by the rapid swirl of this mighty glacier-fed current, sent us sweeping around point after point in rapid succession, and along the lengths of majestic bends. A glorious panorama met our view: Precipitous banks, which the rolling current seemed to hug as it surged past them; then tumbling and flattening hills, which, pressing out, made steppes and terraces and bottoms, forming great points which, shoving the boisterous stream over to the other side, seemed to say to it, "We are not jealous; go and hug the farther bank, as you did us just now;" varied forest foliage, rank, rich prairie grass and luxuriant flora continuously on either bank, fresh from Nature's hand, delightfully arranged, and most pleasing to the eye and to the artistic taste. No wonder I felt glad, for amid these new and glorious scenes, with kind, genial companionship, I was on my way to meet my loved ones, from some of whom I had now been parted more than a year. At night our boats were tied together, and one or two men kept the whole in the current while the others slept. At meal times we put ashore for a few minutes while the kettles were boiled, and then letting the boats float, we ate our meal *en route*.

Early in the middle of the second afternoon we sighted two boats tracking up the southerly bank of the river. Pulling over to intercept them, I was delighted to find my people with them. The Hudson's Bay Company had kindly loaded two boats and sent them on from Carlton, in advance of the brigade, so that father and family should have no delay in reaching their future home. Thanking my friend Hardisty for the very pleasant run of two hundred miles he had given me with him, I transferred to the boat father and mother and my brother and sisters were in. We were very glad to meet again. What sunburnt, but sturdy, happy girls my sisters were! How my baby brother had grown, and now was toddling around like a little man!

Mother was looking forward eagerly to the end of the journey. Already it had occupied a month and more on the way up—half that time in the low country, where water and swamp and muskeg predominate; where flies and mosquitoes flourish and prosper, and reproduce in countless millions; where the sun in the long days of June and July sends an almost unsufferable heat down on the river as it winds its way between low forest-covered banks. The carpenter, Larsen, whom my father was bringing from Norway House, met with an accident, through the careless handling of his gun, and for days and nights mother had to help in nursing and caring for the poor fellow. No wonder she was anxious to reach Victoria, and have change and rest. Forty days and more from Norway House, by lake and river, in open boat—long hot days, long dark, rainy days—with forty very short nights, and yet many of these far too long, because of the never-ceasing mosquito, which, troublesome enough by day, seemed at night to bring forth endless resources of torture, and turn them loose with tireless energy upon suffering humanity. But no one could write up such experiences to the point of realization. You must go through them to know. Mother has had all this, and much more, to endure in her pioneering and missionary life.

Only a day or two before I met them, our folks had the unique sight of witnessing the crossing through the river of thousands of buffalo. The boatmen killed several, and for the time being we were well supplied with fresh meat. Our progress now was very much different to mine coming down. The men kept up a steady tramp, tramp on the bank, at the end of seventy-five or one hundred yards of rope from the boat. Four sturdy fellows in turn kept it up all day, rain or shine, and though our headway was regular, yet because of the interminable windings of the shore, we did not seem to go very far in a day. Several times father and I took across country with our guns, and brought in some ducks and chickens, but the unceasing tramp of the boats' crews did not allow of our going very far from the river.

I think it was the tenth day from my leaving Victoria that I was back again, and Mr. Woolsey welcomed his chairman and colleague with great joy. Mother was not loath to change the York boat for the large buffalo-skin lodge on the banks of the Saskatchewan.

The first thing we went at was hay-making on the old plan, with snath and scythe and wooden forks, and as the weather was propitious we soon had a nice lot of hay put up in good shape; then as father saw at once that the house we were building would take a long time to finish, and as we had some timber in the round on hand, he proposed to at once put up a temporary dwelling-house and a store-house. At this work we went, and Mr. Woolsey looked on in surprise to see these buildings go up as by magic. It was a revelation to him, and to others, the way a man trained in the thick woods of Ontario handled his axe; for, without question, father was one of the best general-purpose axemen I ever came across.

It was my privilege to take a corner on each of these buildings, which is something very different from a corner on wheat or any such thing, but, nevertheless, requires a sharp axe and a steady hand and keen eye; for you must keep your corner square and plumb—conditions which, I am afraid, other cornermen sometimes fail to observe.

Then father sent me up the river with some men to take out timber and to manufacture some lumber for a small church. While we were away on this business, father and Larsen, the carpenter, were engaged in putting the roof on, laying the floors, putting in windows and doors to the log-house, and otherwise getting it ready for occupancy. Despatch was needed, for while a skin lodge may be passable enough for summer, it is a wretchedly cold place in winter, and father was anxious to have mother and the children fairly housed before the cold weather set in.

In the meantime Peter Erasmus had joined our party as father's interpreter and general assistant, and was well to the front in all matters pertaining to the organization of the new mission.

CHAPTER VII.

In search of the Stoneys—An Indian avenger—A Sunday at Fort Edmonton—Drunken Lake carousals—Indian trails—Canyon of the Red Deer—I shoot my father—Amateur surgeons—Prospecting for gold—Peter gets "rattled"—A mysterious shot—Friends or foes?—Noble specimens of the Indian race—A "kodak" needed—Among the Stoneys—Prospecting for a mission site—A massacre of neophytes—An Indian patriarch—Back at Victoria again.

FATHER had been much disappointed at not seeing the Mountain Stoneys on his previous trip west, as time did not permit of his going any farther than Edmonton; but now with temporary house finished, hay made, and other work well on, and as it was still too early to strike for the fresh meat hunt, he determined, with Peter as guide, to make a trip into the Stoney Indian country. Mr. Woolsey's descriptions of his visits to these children of the mountains and forests, of their manly pluck, and the many traits that distinguished them from the other Indians, had made father very anxious to visit them and see what could be done for their present and future good.

Accordingly, one Friday morning early in September, father, Peter and I left the new mission, and taking the bridle trail on the north side, began our journey in search of the Stoneys. We had hardly started when an autumn rainstorm set in, and as our path often led through thick woods, we were soon well soaked and were glad to stop at noon and make a fire to warm and dry ourselves. Continuing our journey, about the middle of the afternoon we came upon a solitary Indian in a dense forest warming himself over a fire, for the rain was cold and had the chill of winter in it.

This Indian proved to be a Plain Cree from Fort Pitt, on the trail of another man who had stolen his wife. He had tracked the guilty pair up the south side to Edmonton, and found that they had gone eastward from there. I told him that a couple had come to Victoria the day before, and he very significantly pointed to his gun and said: "I have that for the man you saw." We left him still warming himself over his fire, and, pushing on, reached Edmonton Saturday evening. Father held two services on Sunday in the officers' mess-room, both well attended.

Monday morning we swam our horses across the Saskatchewan, and crossing ourselves in a small skiff, saddled and packed up, and struck south on what was termed the "Blackfoot Trail." Within ten minutes from leaving the bank of the river we were in a country entirely new to both father and me. We passed Drunken Lake, which Peter told us had been the usual camping-ground of the large trading parties of Indians who periodically came to Edmonton. They would send into the Fort to apprise the officer in charge of their coming to trade. He would then send out to them rum and tobacco, upon which followed a big carousal; then, when through trading, being supplied with more rum, they would come out to this spot, and again go on a big drunk, during which many stabbing and killing scenes were enacted. Thus this lake, on the sloping shores of which these disgraceful orgies had gone on for so long, came to be called Drunken Lake. Fortunately at the time we passed there the Hudson's Bay Company had already given up the liquor traffic in this country among Indians. We passed the spot where Mr. Woolsey and Peter had been held up by a party of Blackfeet, and where for a time things looked very squally, until finally better feelings predominated and the wild fellows concluded to let the "God white man" go with his life and property.

Early in the second day from Edmonton, we left the Blackfoot trail, and started across country, our course being due south. That night we camped at the extreme point of Bear's Hill, and the next evening found us at the Red Deer, near the present crossing, where we found the first signs of Stoneys. The Stoneys made an entirely different trail from that of the Plain Indians. The latter left a broad road because of the *travois* on both dogs and horses, and because of their dragging their lodge poles with them wherever they went. The Stoneys had neither lodge poles nor *travois*, and generally kept in single file, thus making a small, narrow trail, sometimes, according to the nature of the ground, very difficult to trace.

The signs we found indicated that these Indians had gone up the north side of the Red Deer River, so we concluded to follow them, which we did, through a densely wooded country, until they again turned to the river, and crossing it made eastward into a range of hills which stretches from the Red Deer south. In vain we came to camping places one after another. The Indians were gone, and the tracks did not seem to freshen. It was late in the afternoon that the trail brought us down into the canyon of the Red Deer, perhaps twenty miles east of where the railroad now crosses this river. The banks were high, and in some places the view was magnificent. In the long ages past, the then mighty river had burst its way through these hills, and had in time worn its course down to the bed-rock, and in doing so left valleys and flats and canyons to mark its work. In the evolution of things these had become grown over with rich grass and forest timber, and now as we looked, the foliage was changing color, and power and majesty and beauty were before us.

Presently we were at the foot of the long hill, or rather series of hills, and found ourselves on the beach of the river. Peter at once went to try the ford. Father and I sat on our horses side by side, watching him as he struck the current of the stream. Flocks of ducks were flying up and down temptingly near, so father shot at them as he sat on horse-back. I attempted to do the same, but the cap of my gun snapped. I was about to put on another cap when my horse jerked his head down suddenly, and as I had both bridle-lines and gun in the one hand, he jerked them out, and my gun fell on the stones, and, hitting the dog-head, went off. As there was a big rock between my horse and father's, slanting upwards, the discharge of shot bounding from this struck both father and his horse.

"You have hit me, my son!" cried my father.

"Where?" I asked anxiously, as I sprang from

"The discharge of shot, bounding from this, struck both father and his horse." (*Page 70.*)

my horse to my father's side, and as he pointed to his breast, I tore his shirt open, and saw that several pellets had entered his breast.

"Are you hit anywhere else?" I asked; and then he began to feel pain in his leg, and turning up his trousers I found that a number of shot had lodged around the bone in the fleshy part of his leg below the knee.

In the meantime the horse he was riding seemed as if he would bleed to death. His whole breast was like a sieve, and the blood poured in streams from him. Peter saw that something was up and came on the jump through the rapid current, and we bound up father's wounds, turned his horse loose to die—as we thought—and then saddling up another horse for father we crossed the river in order to secure a better place to camp than where we then were. To our astonishment, the horse followed us across, and went to feeding as though nothing had happened.

We at once set to work taking out the pellets of shot. This was of a large size and made quite a wound. We took all out of his chest, and some from his leg, but the rest we could not extract, and father carried them for the rest of his life. We bandaged him with cold water and kept at this, more or less, all next day.

During the intervals of waiting on father, we

burned out our frying-pan, and prospected for gold. We found quite a quantity of colors, but as this was a dangerous country, it being the theatre of constant tribal war, a small party would not be safe to work here very long; so it will be some time before this gold is washed out.

No one can tell how thankful I was that the accident was not worse. The gun was mine; the fault, if any there were, was mine. With mingled feelings of sorrow and gladness, I passed the long hours of that first night after the accident. Father was in great pain at times, but cold water was our remedy, and by the morning of the second day we moved camp out of the canyon up to near the mouth of the Blind Man's River.

The next morning we were up early, and while I brought the horses in, father and Peter had determined our course. I modestly enquired where we were going, and they told me their plan was to come out at a place on our outbound trail, which we had named Goose Lakes, because of having dined on goose at that place. I ventured to give my opinion that the course they pointed out would not take us there, but in an altogether different direction. However, as it turned out, Peter was astray that morning, and got turned around, as will sometimes happen with the best of guides. After travelling for some time in the wrong direction, as we were about to enter a range of thickly-wooded hills, the brush of which hurt father very much, I ventured to again suggest we were out of our way. Peter then acknowledged he was temporarily "rattled," and asked me to go ahead, which I did, retracing our track out of the timber, and then striking straight for the Goose Lakes, where we came out upon our own trail about noon. After that both father and Peter began to appreciate my pioneering instincts as not formerly.

Most of this time we had been living on our guns. In starting we had a small quantity of flour, about two pounds of which was now left in the little sack in which we carried it.

Saturday afternoon we crossed Battle River, and arranging to camp at the "Leavings," that is, at a point where the trail which in after years was made between Edmonton and Southern Alberta, touched and left the Battle River, Peter followed down the river to look for game, while father and I went straight to the place where we intended to camp. Our intention was to not travel on Sunday, if we could in the meantime obtain a supply of food. Reaching this place, father said to me, "Never mind the horses, but start at once and see what you can do for our larder." I exchanged guns with father, as his was a double barrel and mine a single, and ran off to the river, where I saw a fine flock of stock ducks. Firing into them, I brought down two. Almost immediately I heard the report of a gun away down the river, and father called to me, "Did you hear that?" I said "Yes." Then he said, "Fire off the second barrel in answer," which I did, and there came over the hill the sound of another shot. Then we knew that people were near, but who they were was the question which interested us very much. By this time I had my gun loaded, and the ducks got out of the river, and had run back to father. Peter came up greatly excited, asking us if we had heard the shots. We explained that two came from us, and the others from parties as yet unknown to us. "Then," said he, "we will tie our horses, and be ready for either friends or foes."

Presently we were hailed from the other bank of the river, and looking over we saw, peering from out the bush, two Indians, who proved to be Stoneys. When Peter told them who we were, there was mutual joy, and they at once plunged into the river, and came across to us. Their camp, they informed us, was near, and when we told them we were camped for Sunday, they said they would go back and bring up their lodges and people to where we were. They told us, moreover, that there were plenty of provisions in their camp, that they had been fortunate in killing several elk and deer very recently—all of which we were delighted to hear.

If these had been the days of the "kodak," I would have delighted in catching the picture of those young Indians as they stood before us, exactly fitting into the scene which in its immensity and isolation lay all around us. Both were fine looking men. Their long black hair, in two neat braids, hung pendant down their breasts. The middle tuft was tied up off the forehead by small strings of ermine skin. Their necks were encircled with a string of beads, with a sea-shell immediately under the chin. A small thin, neatly made and neatly fitting leather shirt, reaching a little below the waist; a breech cloth, fringed leather leggings, and moccasins, would make up the costume; but these were now thrown over their shoulders as they crossed the river. Strong and well-built, with immense muscular development in the lower limbs, showing that they spent most of the time on their feet, and had climbed many a mountain and hill, as they stood there with their animated and joyous faces fairly beaming with satisfaction because of this glad meeting, and that the missionary and his party were going to stay some time with them and their people, they looked true specimens of the aboriginal man, and almost, or altogether (it seemed to me) just where the Great Spirit intended them to be. I could not help but think of the fearful strain, the terrible wrenching out of the very roots of being of the old life, there must take place before these men would become what the world calls civilized.

Away bounded our visitors, and in a very short time our camp was a busy scene. Men, women, and children, dogs and horses! We were no more isolate and alone. Provisions poured in on us, and our commissariat was secure for that trip. To hold meetings, to ask and answer questions, to sit up late around the open camp-fire in the business of the Master, to get up early Sunday morning and hold services and catechize and instruct all the day until bedtime again came, was the constant occupation and joy of the missionary, and no man I ever travelled with seemed to enter into such work and be better fitted for it than my father. Though he never attempted to speak in the language of the Indian, yet few men knew how to use an interpreter as he did, and Peter was then and is now no ordinary interpreter.

These Indians told us that the Mountain Stoneys were away south at the time, and that there would be no chance of our seeing them on this trip; that in all probability they would see the Mountain Indians during the coming winter, and would gladly carry to them any messages father might have to send. Father told them to tell their people that (God willing) he would visit their camps next summer; that they might be gathered and on the look-out for himself and party sometime during the "Egg Moon." He discussed with them the best site for a mission, if one should be established for them and their people. There being two classes of Stoneys, the Mountain and the Wood, it was desirable to have the location central. The oldest man in the party suggested Battle River Lake, the head of the stream on which we were encamped, and father determined to take this man as guide and explore the lake.

Monday morning found us early away, after public prayer with the camp, to follow up the river to its source. Thomas, our guide for the trip to the lake, was one of those men who are instinctively religious. He had listened to the first missionary with profound interest, and presently, finding in this new faith that which satisfied his hungry soul, embraced it with all his heart. Thus we found him in his camp when first we met, and thus I have always found the faithful fellow, during thirty-two years of intimate knowledge and acquaintance with him.

We saw the lake, and stood on the spot where some of Rundle's neophytes were slaughtered by their enemies. This bloody act had nipped in the bud the attempt of Benjamin Sinclair, under Mr. Rundle, to establish a mission on the shore of Pigeon Lake, only some ten miles from the scene of the massacre, and drove Ben and his party over two hundred miles farther into the northern country. We were three days of steady travelling on this side trip, and reached our camp late the evening of the third day.

Two more services with this interesting people, and bidding them good-bye, we started for home by a different route from that by which we had come. Going down Battle River, we passed outside the Beaver Hills, skirted Beaver Lake, and passing through great herds of buffalo without firing a shot—because we had provisions given us by the Indians—we found ourselves, at dusk Saturday night, about thirty-five miles from Victoria. Continuing our journey until after midnight, we unsaddled, and waited for the Sabbath morning light to go on into the mission.

Early in the morning, as we were now about ten miles from home, we came upon a solitary lodge, and found there, with his family, "Old Stephen," another of the early converts of our missionaries. I had often heard Mr. Woolsey speak of the old man, but had never met him before. As he stood in the door of his tent, leaning on his staff, with his long white hair floating in the breeze, he looked a patriarch indeed. We alighted from our horses, and after singing a hymn father led in prayer. Old Stephen was profoundly affected at meeting with father. He welcomed him to the plains and the big Saskatchewan country, and prayed that his coming might result in great good.

As we were mounting our horses to leave him, the old man said: "Yes, with you it is different; you have God's Word, can read it, and understand it. I cannot read, nor do I understand very much, but I am told that God said, 'Keep the praying day holy,' and, therefore, wherever the evening of the day before the praying day finds me, I camp until the light of the day after the praying day comes," and fully appreciating the old man's consistency, we also could not help but feel rebuked, though we were in time for morning service at the mission, and home again once more.

CHAPTER VIII.

Provisions diminishing—A buffalo hunt organized—Oxen and Red River carts—Our "buffalo runners"—Meet with Maskepetoon—Maskepetoon shakes hands with his son's murderer—An Indian's strange vow—Instance of Indian watchfulness—"Who-Talks-Past-All-Things"—Come upon the buffalo—An exciting charge—Ki-you-ken-os races the buffalo—Peter's exciting adventure—Buffalo dainties—Return home—War parties—Indian curiosity—Starving Young Bull's "dedication feast"—Missionary labors.

DRIED meat and pemmican, with fowl and fish now and then, make very good food, but when you have no vegetables or flour to give variety, you are apt to become tired of them. Our garden on the new land had done very well, but it was a mere bite for the many mouths it had to fill. Our own party was large, and then every little while starving Indians and passing travellers would call, and these must be fed. There was no Hudson's Bay post nearer than Edmonton and no stores. The new mission, already in its first season, had become the house of refuge for quite a number, both red and white.

As near as I can remember, it was about the

first of October that we organized our party for the plains. To do this there was a lot of work to be done in preparation—horses to hunt up, carts to mend, old axles to replace with new ones, harness to fix. We had one waggon. The rest of our vehicles were of the old Red River pattern, wood through and through, that screamed as it rolled. Some of these wanted new felloes, and others new spokes; another had a broken shaft. Then when all was ready we had the river to cross, and our only means of ferriage was a small skiff. This involved many trips, and when all the carts and our one waggon were over, then came the work of swimming our stock across. With the horses we had but little difficulty, but the oxen were loath to take the water, and we had to lead them over one by one. Then when all were across and hitched up, we had the big hill to pull up; for while the north bank of the Saskatchewan at this point has a naturally easy approach, the south bank is almost perpendicular. Even to-day, notwithstanding considerable grading, it is a bad hill, but at the time I write of we had to double up our teams to take a light cart to the summit.

Mr. Woolsey remained in charge of the mission. Father was captain of the hunting party, with Erasmus second in command. The rest of us were teamsters, or guards, or privates, as the need might be. On the second day out we met the vanguard of Maskepetoon's camp on their way to the mission. From them we learned the glad news that we might expect to find buffalo about the fifth day out, or possibly sooner.

Our rate of travel was governed by the oxen, but as we started very early and travelled late, we could cover a long distance in a day. In going out I drove the waggon and went ahead. Our "runners" ran and fed beside us as we travelled. Father and Peter were in the saddle, and drove up the loose stock, or were anywhere on the line of march as need might require.

The buffalo runners need especial mention. There was Peter's horse, a handsome little roan, full of spirit, and yet gentle and easy to manage. Then there was old "Ki-you-ken-os," a big bay that had evidently been stolen from the Americans to the south and had been brought into Edmonton by a Blackfoot, after whom the horse was named. Later on he had come into Mr. Woolsey's hands, and thus we had him with us. He was a fine animal, but altogether too impetuous and strong-mouthed to make a good buffalo horse. I saw him run away with father one day, and although father was an exceptionally strong man, he had to let him go; he could not stop him, pull as he might. Then there was my saddle-horse, "The Scarred Thigh," as the Indians called him, because a mad bull had torn him with his horn. A fine little sorrel he was, and an A1 buffalo horse. These we seldom touched on the journey, except to give them a short run by way of exercise and to keep them in wind.

About the middle of the afternoon of the second day out, we met Maskepetoon himself. He was delighted to again see father, and said he would send some of his young men with us to help in the hunt, as also to help guard our camp and party. For this purpose the old gentleman got into my waggon and rode with me a mile or two, to where the Indians were that he wanted to send with us. As we drove on, we kept meeting Indians, and Maskepetoon told me who they were, and introduced me to several. Presently I saw an old man, of singular appearance, approaching, and I said to Maskepetoon, "Who is that?" But he, when he saw who it was, did not reply, but turned the other way, which I thought strange. The old man came up to my side of the waggon, and said: "I am glad to see you, young white man." So we shook hands; and he made as if he would shake hands with the man beside me, for I knew he did not recognize Maskepetoon, not expecting to see him in my waggon, and going this way. The chief still kept his face turned away. I saw, however, that after shaking my hand, the old man would also shake hands with my companion, so I nudged Maskepetoon and said, "This man wants to shake hands with you." Then the chief, as if jerking himself from under a weight or strain, turned and gave his hand to the old fellow, who, on recognizing him grasped his hand and uttered the Indian form of thanksgiving, doing this in solemn earnest.

It was some time before Maskepetoon spoke to me again: "John, that man killed my son, and I have often longed to kill him; but because I have wanted to embrace the Christian religion, I have with great effort kept from avenging my son's murder. I have never spoken to him or shaken hands with him until now. Meeting your father and sitting beside you has softened my heart, and now I have given him my hand. It was a hard thing to do, but it is done, and he need fear no longer so far as I am concerned."

Later on, I found out that the man we saw and Maskepetoon's son had gone across the mountains to trade horses from the Kootenays, and on the return trip the old man had killed his companion, and given out that he had been attacked by other Indians; but afterwards it was found out that he had done the foul deed himself. No wonder my friend felt strongly. Any man would in such a case. Rundle and Woolsey and Steinhauer had not preached in vain, when such evidence of the lodgment of the Gospel seed was so distinctly apparent.

Presently we came to the Indians Maskepetoon was in search of. He sent four with us—his son Joseph, his nephew Jack, a Blood man, and a Swamptree—fine fellows every one of them. Joseph was big, solid and staid—a man you could depend on. Jack was small, quick and wild—fond of war and given to excess. It was a long time before he gave up horse-stealing and polygamy. The Blood and the Swamptree were both typical wood and plain Indians, pagans still, but instinctively kind and well disposed. I had met all four several times during the previous year. They all had great respect for father, and would with alacrity seek to anticipate his wish while with us. The Blood man was under vows to his "familiar spirit," or "the one he dreams of," and one of the injunctions laid upon him was to give a whoop every little while, a very peculiar semi-peace, semi-war whoop. He said to me, in confidence, "John, you do not mind me, but I dare not make my whoop before your father. That is why I go away from camp now and then. I must whoop; it would choke me, kill me, if I did not." I told him to "whoop it up." I saw no harm in it, and the poor fellow was comforted.

As a sample of the trained watchfulness of the men, I must relate an incident that occurred on our journey. The Swamptree was riding in the waggon with father and myself. On the fourth day out we were passing through bluffs of timber, thickly dotting the prairie, when suddenly I saw the Swamptree string his bow and throw an arrow into position in a flash. So quickly did he do this that I was startled, and exclaimed, "What do you see back there?" The answer, "Men!" came in a quiet tone, almost a whisper. "Where?" I asked. "At that point of bushes is one," said he. Looking to where he indicated I caught the glint of an eye, and telling father, our guns were soon brought to bear on the crouching Indian, who, seeing he was discovered, rose, with his hand up. Our friend recognized him as a Cree, and behind him stood a noted character who went by the name of "Who-Talks-Past-All-Things." He had French blood, was a Roman Catholic, and spent most of his time around the Roman Catholic missions. He sometimes imagined himself to be the Pope, and very often officiated among the Indians as priest. He had come out this time with a team and waggon from the Roman Catholic mission at Big Lake for a load of fresh meat, and was now returning. He and his companion were camped for dinner on the other side of the bluff of timber. They had heard us coming, and were bound to make sure who we were before showing themselves.

They told us of buffalo, and we went on gladly; but as we were now outside of the Wood Cree camps we kept a sharp lookout for enemies, and a constant guard at night. The next day—the fifth out from the mission—we sighted buffalo, in "bunches" or bands, about noon. We had been seeing a few all morning, mostly bulls, but we were after cow meat, and about noon saw several bunches not far from us. The country was of a very rolling nature, and about half and half prairie and brush. Jack and Joseph and Peter and I saddled and made ready to run. Peter took Ki-you-ken-os and putting a big curb-bit in his mouth, I heard him say to the horse, "I will be bound to hold you with this." The rest of our party stayed with the carts.

We charged at the buffalo as they were running down the slope of a hill towards an opening between two dense thickets of timber. The last I saw of Peter was when two bands of buffalo were meeting in their mad rush for this opening, and old Ki-you-ken-os seemed determined to take the gap before them. Peter had his gun stuck in his belt, had hold of the double reins from the big curb-bit with both hands, and was pulling with all his might, mouth wide open, and eyes bulging out; but the old horse did not seem to heed either Peter or his bit—he was running the buffalo a race for yonder gap. Peter and his horse were on the centre line of three converging forces: two bands of buffalo, perhaps two hundred in each, and Peter and his wild horse. I fully expected to see some buffalo killed by the collision, which was inevitable. I was terribly anxious for Peter. In a few moments the two herds came against each other. A moment later the horse and his rider were in the centre of the confused mass, and then all I could see was buffalo stampeding, and old Ki-you-ken-os leaping over and running amongst the wild herd, which was now tightly jamming its way through the narrow prairie lane. Then dust and distance hid the scene from me.

This was my second run after buffalo. My first shot was a miss, and loading again I fired, only to miss again. I blamed badger-holes and brush and dust, but lack of experience was what did it. I had killed in my first race, but did not in my second. My horse was good, my gun, though single shot, was sure. It was my fault, and I felt it keenly. Peter also did not kill in that race—indeed, he was thankful, as was I, that he was not killed; but Joseph and Jack made up for it, and we were busy all the rest of the evening butchering and hauling in to where we camped for the night.

We were now in the short day and long night season, which in these northern latitudes is especially marked. Moreover the nights were cold, and we must have a big camp-fire. So we got well down between the bluffs, in order that the glare of our fire would be hidden as much as possible, and arranged our carts around the camp so that these would act as a kind of barricade in case of attack. Tying our oxen up to ruminate on the grass they had eaten this day, and fall back on the fat they had made during the summer, we tethered our horses close, and alternating on guard over them, the balance busied themselves around the camp, putting away the meat and cooking supper.

This latter process took hours to get through with, for everybody had his choice bit to roast. The cook for the evening would have a whole side of ribs swinging before the fire, and when these were cooked the ribs were parted along the whole length, and each man took one. When he had picked it clean he either turned his attention to his own independent roast, or took another rib. One had brought the head in, though generally when you took the tongue out you left the head for the wolves. Another had two or three fathoms of entrails, which he cleaned with fire, and then roasted, and cutting them up in lengths, passed these around to his friends. Another had a large piece of the stomach or tripe, which he also cleaned with fire, and relished as a favorite morsel. Still another was cracking marrow bones, and eating the marrow. Thus supper was prolonged far beyond the usual time. When those whose turn it was to sleep felt it was bed-time, we would sing a hymn, and father lead in prayer, then the bed-making began. With old hands this commenced by piling saddles and camp equipment, or logs of wood, behind the head and on each side of where you were going to sleep, for experience had taught these wary fellows that many a bullet and arrow had been stopped, or made to glance off, by such simple precautions. Fresh guards set, the rest lay down with clothes and moccasins on, so as to be ready to jump at any time, having carefully looked to arms before doing so.

The next day we finished loading up and started homewards, but had not gone far when one of the oxen, with his heavily loaded cart, ran foul of our waggon and broke one of its axles. Fortunately there were some birch trees about a couple of miles from us, and father and one of the Indians rode over, and brought two sticks capable of being made into axles. An accident of this kind under ordinary circumstances would be a small thing, but with our lack of tools it meant something to fit a waggon axle. However, Peter and father fixed it up, and on we went, travelling early and late, which, by the way, is no light work, but sometimes exceedingly hard on flesh and blood. To start out from your camp-fire long before daylight on a cold, frosty morning, and perhaps have to break the new-made ice on some creek by jumping into it yourself in order to lead your carts safely across, and then to go on wet as well as cold—I say again, that this was felt to be very hard work by some of our party. Nevertheless, doing it, and keeping at it, we were back at the Saskatchewan on the thirteenth day from the start. Then we had to unload and take everything over in a small skiff, reload again and haul up to our staging, which at this season was a better place to keep the meat than in a store-house.

A great change had come over the place since we left. Hundreds of lodges now dotted the valley, and Mr. Woolsey and Maskepetoon had been very busy keeping the camp in order. A great many Plain Crees were here mixed up with our quieter Wood Crees, and war parties were coming and going all the time. Mother and my sisters, though among Indians for many years—in fact, the girls had spent all their lives among them—had never seen anything like this before. Men and women would crowd around the little temporary mission house, and in full savage costume, and with faces painted in divers colors, peer into the windows, and darken the door, and look with the greatest curiosity on the white woman and her children.

Paganism was rife. Conjuring and gambling were going on night and day. Dance feasts, and dog feasts, and wolf feasts, and new lodge dedication feasts were everyday occurrences. I was invited to join in one of the latter, by a Plain Cree, a warrior and a polygamist, and a dandy of the first circle, who had taken a fancy for me. His name was peculiar, and he, being a sleek and fine-looking fellow, most certainly belied it. "The Starving Young Bull" was the gentleman who honored me with an invitation to be present at the dedication feast of his new lodge, now about finished; and these new lodges were gorgeous things in their way. The twenty or more buffalo skins had been dressed soft and white as possible and then cut into shape by some pattern carried in the brain of one of the older women; then at a bee of women, where also a feast was provided, the skins were sewn together with the sinews of the buffalo, and when the new tent, tasseled with the tail of the same animal, was fully set, then the artist friends, or the proprietor himself, went to work to paint upon its outside walls the achievements of the warrior and hunter—scenes of plunder, blood, etc., military prowess, medicinal lore—so that in approaching a tent you could read the degree and dignity of the man you were about to visit.

I accepted Mr. Starving Young Bull's kind invitation, and was on hand at the time he had indicated. "Just as the day is departing," was the hour he fixed. There may have been forty or more guests. We sat in a ring around the tent. Each man had before him his own dish, which he had brought with him, and when these had been heaped up with buffalo dainties and dried berries, four old conjurers, who sat at the head of the tent, each dressed in accord with the instructions of the "spirit of his dream," now began the dedication service. First the oldest conjurer took the big medicine pipe, with the long stem. This had been previously filled, and as he solemnly held it in both hands, another with his knife placed a live coal on the contents of the pipe. This done, the old man pulled at it until it was fairly alight, and then held the stem heavenwards, at the same time muttering what to us were unintelligible sounds. Next he pointed the stem to the earth, then slowly moved it around with the sun, and taking another whiff or two, passed it to his fellow-conjurers, who each in turn took long pulls at the big pipe. After this the four took their sacred rattles and began to sing and incant, keeping time with the rattles. Then they all began to speak in an unknown language, or as it is literally translated, "using a different language." When through with this, the old man in the language of the people (which I could understand) offered up a prayer—or rather expressed a wish—"that this tent might be blessed; that "its occupants might be prospered; that the " owner, in his going out and coming in, whether " for hunting or war, might be successful; that "the kettles of the women of this tent might " always boil with plenty; that the pipe of the " owner might always be full;" all of which was responded to by the guests. Then we devoted ourselves to the feast, eating much or little as we chose, and taking home with us what we did not eat.

In the midst of all these old institutions and

rites, which these people had been bred in for centuries, our missionaries were hard at work, sowing the seeds of a brighter and better faith. Meetings and councils followed each other in quick succession, and early and late father and Mr. Woolsey were busy preaching the Gospel of Christianity and civilization to these men to whom they had been sent. In all this they were nobly backed by Maskepetoon, and such men as Stephen, and his son Joseph, Thomas Woolsey—a fine fellow, to whom Mr. Woolsey had given his name—and others who had already experienced the religion of the Lord Jesus, and were going on to know more of it.

CHAPTER IX.

The fall fishing—A relentless tooth-ache—Prairie and forest fire—Attacked by my dogs—A run home—A sleepless night—Father turns dentist—Another visit to Edmonton—Welcome relief—Final revenge on my enemy.

IN the meantime we were putting up stables and out-buildings, and going on with work on the mission house. We also put up the walls of a small church. Then the time came to look after the fall fishing, and we concluded to go to Saddle Lake for this purpose. Upon me fell the work of establishing the fishery, and to me was given as companion and fellow-worker a young Canadian, Thomas Kernan by name. Our plan was to go down the river in the skiff, as far as the Snake Hills, which were about opposite the lake, and then portage our boat over the hills the eight or ten miles to the lake. Peter was to meet us at the place of landing, and we took with us in our boat a pair of cart-wheels, on which to transport our boat from the river to the lake. An axe and an auger were all the tools we had. We took a skin lodge to live in at the fishery, and embarking one afternoon came to the place of meeting early the next day. Peter turned up in convenient time with a horse, and we went to work to make a frame and axle for the wheels, and soon had our boat loaded on this with our fishing outfit, tent, etc., and were tramping up the hills. On the way we killed five large geese and some ducks, and were at the lake in time to put up our tent and set one net that night, Peter being anxious to taste the fish before he returned to the mission.

Peter had not to wait until the next morning for his fish, for we caught some that very night, and had them cooked for our second supper. He returned home the following day —some forty miles straight across country— and Tom and I were left to go on with our fishing operations. Making floats, tying stones, setting nets, putting up fish, taking up the nets, washing and drying and mending them, and resetting them—all this kept us busy from daylight until nine o'clock at night. Tom had never done any such work before, but he was teachable and diligent, and proved a splendid companion. All this time, however, I was in perfect misery with one of my teeth. It had been aching for over two months, and had, in a large measure, taken the pleasure out of all my later trips. Whether hunting the Stoneys, chasing buffalo, or at home at Victoria, that old tooth kept on the jump and made life miserable. I had burned it with a red-hot iron, had poulticed it, had done everything I could, but as there was not a pair of forceps in the country, I could not have it pulled. Now the overhauling of nets morning and night, working in the cold water, was making my tooth worse than ever. Sometimes I was almost distracted with the gnawing ache and pain.

One day we had an experience which made me forget my tooth for the time. A great prairie and forest fire suddenly came sweeping down upon us. We had very little time to roll the tent up on the poles, gather our bedding and nets, our guns, ammunition, etc., into the boat, and shove off, before the fire was upon us. We got out to one of our net sticks, and I held on to it while the smoke and flame and the intense heat lasted. Sometimes I was so nearly choking that I almost let go my hold. Had I lost my grip, this would have run us into another danger, a high wind having risen by this time. Our dogs must have taken to the water also, for when the smoke had cleared away they were on the spot waiting for us.

Some days later these very dogs made me again forget the tooth-ache for a little while. We had a small ham of buffalo meat left, which

"To save my life I had to climb to the top of the staging."
(*Page 99.*)

we were saving for Sundays and special occasions. Coming ashore one day I noticed fresh bones near the tent, and looking up on the stage where our meat ought to have been, I saw that the dogs had somehow or other got hold of it. This so incensed me that I determined to thrash everyone of them. I caught the one I knew to be the biggest thief of the lot, but at the first slap I gave him the whole pack of ten big dogs sprang at me. I might have fought them off if all had attacked me from one direction, but they came from all sides, and to save my life I had to climb to the top of the staging. In a flash I was occupying the place vacated by our unfortunate ham, and not until Tom, who was down at the lake cleaning fish, came to my rescue and whistled the dogs off, did I dare to leave my perch of safety. A long summer's idleness, and now being fat and strong, had made these dogs savage, but they came under all right when we began to work them.

All this time my tooth was getting worse, and after putting in a terrible night, I said to Tom: "Are you willing to stay here alone while I go to the mission and see if I cannot in some way obtain relief from this tooth?" and the plucky fellow said, "Go ahead, John, and I will do the best I can until you send some one to help me." So away I ran, with only a light coat on, and but a small piece of dried meat stuck into my bosom. Of course I had my gun and some matches, but I fully expected to reach the mission that evening. I did not know how nearly used up I was by those days and nights of intense suffering. Before I had gone very far I began to lag. Then there was no road to follow, and never having been across that way before, I went too much to the north, was cut off my course by a chain of lakes, and had to retrace my way for a long distance.

Evening came on, and with it cold and storm. I saw I would have to camp out. Sighting a fall duck, which was staying up in these latitudes longer than most of its kind, I shot it, and waded out after it up to my waist with clothes and all on, but finding the water deepening, I was forced after all to abandon my bird. Then, with clothes frozen, I travelled on in wretched discomfort until, darkness coming on, I camped in the lee of some scrub pines. Making a fire, I prepared to spend another even more miserable night, for with the tooth-ache there was now the undesirable accompaniment of cold, hunger and loneliness.

As night wore on the storm increased, and the wind from the north grew bitterly cold. I was extremely glad that some of the dogs had followed me; and after drying my clothes I took two of the animals, and tying them together with my belt, I stretched them at my back, and, with the fire on one side and the dogs on the other, tried to get the much-needed rest and sleep. But between the cold and that relentless molar, there was no sleep to be had. Piling on the wood, I shivered and suffered over that fire through the long, tedious night. It was with great relief I saw the first glimmer of coming day; but not until it was fairly light did I venture forth, for I did not care to run any more risks as to my course. I was now both hungry and weak; and thus I travelled on until a little after sunrise, when I saw some horses ahead of me. While wondering how I might catch one, I came in sight of two lodges, and making for them, found that one of them belonged to the "Blood" man whom I have already introduced to my readers. He received me kindly, and fed me hospitably. He and the people in the other lodges were on their way to the lake where we had been fishing, and I begged them to hurry on, for my companion was there alone. Refreshed by the hearty breakfast, and having the track of this party to guide me, I then pursued my journey. I had still twenty miles to make. This in ordinary times with me would have been but a little run, but now it seemed a fearful distance. I fairly dragged my legs along, and was almost thoroughly played out when at last, late in the evening, I reached the mission. Father was away at Edmonton. Mother did all she could for me, but that tireless tooth simply ached on; there was no stopping it. When father came home, Peter, who was with him, went right on to the fishing to take my place, while father got a pair of pinchers, and, with the aid of the carpenter, Larsen, filed them into the shape of forceps. With this improvised instrument he set to work to extract the tooth, but after five fruitless efforts at this, he broke the tooth off square with the gums, and then it ached worse than ever!

Winter had now set in, and the river soon was frozen over, so as to admit of travel. Mr. Woolsey having business at Edmonton, I took him with cariole and dogs, following the ice all the way there and back. That tooth kept up its aching, more or less, all the time until we came within thirty miles of home. The last day of the trip, while we were having lunch, I was eating a piece of pemmican, when all of a sudden my tooth stopped aching. I felt a hole in it, and also felt something queer in my mouth. Taking this out, I found it to be a piece of the nerve. The pain was gone, and my relief may be imagined. I think I must have gained about ten pounds in weight within the next two weeks. I owe it to dental history to record that nine years after, when paying my first flying visit to Ontario, I sat down in cold blood and told the dentist to dig out those roots; for verily there was deep rooted in me the desire for revenge on that tooth. He did dig it out, and I was pleased and satisfied to part with my old enemy.

CHAPTER X.

Casual visitors—The missionary a "medicine man"—"Hardy dogs and hardier men"—A buffalo hunt organized—"Make a fire! I am freezing!"—I thaw out my companion—Chief Child—Father caught napping—Go with Mr. Woolsey to Edmonton—Encounter between Blackfeet and Stoneys—A "nightmare" scare—My passenger scorched—Rolling down hill—Translating hymns.

WITH the first approach of winter, the majority of the Indians re-crossed the Saskatchewan and pitched southward for buffalo. Some waited until the ice-bridge was formed, and a few went northward into the woods to trap and hunt for fur; but it rarely happened that there were no Indians about the place. Strangers, having heard that missionaries were settling on the river near the "Hairy Bag," (which was the old name for a valley just back of the mission house, given to it because it had been a favorite feeding-ground for buffalo) would come out of their way to camp for a day or two beside the new mission, and see for themselves what was going on and what was the purpose of such effort. Many a seed of truth found lodgment in the hearts of these wanderers, to bear rich fruit in soul-winning in later days.

Then the missionary became noted as a "medicine man," able to help the divers diseased. Many of these were brought from afar that they might reap the benefit of his care. Then all the hungry and naked hunters, those out of luck, upon whom some spell had been cast (as they believed) so that their nets failed to catch, their guns missed fire, and their traps snapped, or their dead-falls fell without trapping anything—where else should these unfortunates go for help and advice and comfort but to the "praying man." And thus with our large party, and the very many other calls upon our commissariat, it kept some of us on the jump to gather provisions sufficient to "keep the pot boiling."

Already, because of the snow coming earlier, we had hauled most of our fish from the lake, fairly rushing things after we had the road broken. Generally two trips were made in three days, and now and then a trip a day. Away at two or three o'clock in the morning; forty miles out light, then lashing a hundred or more frozen whitefish on our narrow dog-sled, and home again the same evening with the load, yoked to hardy dogs and still hardier men. One such trip was enough for any weakling or faint-heart who might try it.

Owing to the great demands upon our larder, already referred to, early in December of this winter (1863) we found our supply of fresh meat nearly exhausted, and so determined to go out in search of a fresh supply. Already a good foot of snow was on the ground around Victoria, and there was more south and east, where the Indians and buffalo were, but this did not stop us from starting out. The party consisted of father, Peter, Tom, a man named Johnson, and myself. We took both horses and dogs. The second day out we encountered intensely cold weather, and this decided us to strike eastward into the hills along the south of the chain of lakes. The third day we killed two bulls, and as the meat was very good, father told Tom and I to load our sleds and return to the mission, and to come right back again.

Off we started with our loads, but as we had a road to break across country our progress was slow. We had no snowshoes, and I had to wade ahead of the dogs, while Tom brought up the rear. That night was one of the coldest in my experience, and I know what cold means if any man does. Tom and I had each a small blanket. We made as good a camp as we could by clearing away the snow and putting down a

"I got Tom up, and held him close over the fire." (*Page 107.*)

lot of frozen willows. We kept up a good fire, but the heat did not seem to have any radiating power that night—an almost infinite wall of frosty atmosphere was pressing in on us from all sides. Putting our unlined capotes beneath and the two blankets over us, we tried to sleep, for we had travelled steadily and worked hard all the day. I went to sleep, but Tom shivered beside me, and presently woke me up by exclaiming: "John, for God's sake make a fire! I am freezing!" I hurried as fast as I could, and soon had a big blaze going. Then I got Tom up and held him close over the fire, rubbing and chafing, and turning him all the while, until the poor fellow was somewhat restored. Looking gratefully at me, he then noticed that I had neither coat nor mitts on. I had not felt the need of these, so startled and anxious was I because of my comrade's condition. We did not try to sleep any more that night, but busied ourselves in chopping and carrying logs for our fire, and religiously keeping this up.

With the first glimmer of day we were away, and steadily kept our weary wading through the deep, loose snow. About eight in the evening we came out on the trail leading to the mission, and would have been home by midnight, only that I had to make another fire about ten o'clock, and give Tom another thawing out to save his life. He was a slight, slim fellow, and the bitter cold seemed to go right through him; but he was a lad of real grit and true pluck.

Fortunately for Tom and I, it was between two and three o'clock Sunday morning when we reached the mission. This gave us the day's rest, otherwise we would have felt in duty bound to turn right around and go back to our party. Our people at home were glad to have the fresh meat, and though Mr. Woolsey had then spent eight years among the buffalo, he pronounced it "good cow's meat." We concluded thereupon that at any rate it was extra good "bull's meat," and were satisfied with our part of the work.

A little after midnight Tom and I set forth on our return. The cold was intense, but we were light, and running and riding we made a tremendous day of it, coming about noon to where we had parted from our friends. Following them up we came to where they had found the trail of an Indian camp, and gone on it. Carrying on, we camped when night came, and as we had now a distinct trail, we left our camp in the night, and a little after daylight had the satisfaction of seeing the white smoke from many lodges rising high into the cold, clear air in the distance. This stimulated us, and within two hours we were in the camp and again with our friends. They had fallen in with a party of Indians from Whitefish Lake and north of it, and father and party were now in Chief Child's lodge. Both missionary and people had been having a good time together. These simple people, having been reached by the Gospel, and having accepted the truth, were never happier than when receiving an unexpected visit from a missionary. When the missionary delighted in his work and made himself as interesting as possible to the people, and spared no pains to make his visit profitable and educative, as father always did, then their satisfaction knew no bounds. With their teacher they all became optimistic, hopeful, and joyous.

Father told me that Chief Child, our host, had given him some of the finest meat he had ever eaten, and that our hostess knew how to cook buffalo meat to perfection. Now, as my experience amongst buffalo-eating Indians was one year older than father's, I began to suspect that he had been caught napping, and had eaten what he would not have indulged in had he known; so I quietly enquired of Chief Child what he had fed father on. He replied, "We have no variety. He has had nothing but buffalo meat in my tent;" then, as if correcting himself, he added, "Perhaps it was the unborn calf meat he found so good." Just as I thought, said I to myself; now I have a good one on father! Later on, when he repeatedly spoke of Chief Child's hospitality, I mentioned this, and father opened his eyes, then quite philosophically said, "Can't help it—it was delicious anyway."

Father and party were about ready to start back when we reached the camp, having secured fine loads of both fresh and dried meats, so we loaded up and started for home. As we with the dog-trains could travel faster, and make longer distances than the horses, Peter and Tom and I went on, leaving father and Johnson to come as they could. We were home, and had made another trip to the fishery and back, by the time they got in with their loads.

Mr. Woolsey was now ready to set out on the missionary tour to Edmonton, usually taken during the holidays. It had become an established custom for the officers and employees of the Hudson's Bay Company who desired to come to Edmonton on business or pleasure to do so at that time, and the missionary had then the opportunity of meeting people from the outposts as well as those resident in the Fort.

In accord with this purpose we left Victoria in time to reach Edmonton the day before Christmas. I drove the cariole as usual, and we had with us a newcomer, one "Billy" Smith, a man we had known at Norway House, and who had now, somehow or other, drifted into this upper country. Billy drove the baggage and "grub train." Simultaneous with our starting for Edmonton, father, Peter and the others also set out to procure, if possible, another load of meat, as there was no telling where the buffalo might be driven to in a short time.

We went by the south side, taking the route I had followed on my lone trip, and arrived at Edmonton on time. Remaining there during the holiday week, we started back the day after New Year's. While we were there a small party of Mountain Stoneys came in on a trade to the Fort. With these was Jonas, one of Rundle's converts, who understood Cree well, and Mr. Woolsey arranged with him to return with us to Victoria, as father and he were very desirous of securing the translation of some hymns into Stoney. Thus our party was augmented by Jonas and a companion. The rest of this small party of Stoneys, on their return trip south, were attacked by the Blackfeet when about fifty miles from the Fort, and several were killed and wounded on both sides; but the Stoneys, though much outnumbered, eventually succeeded in driving their enemies away. It may be that Jonas saved his life that time by coming with our company.

Just as we were starting from Edmonton, Billy Smith was bitten in the hand by one of the dogs. The wound became very bad almost immediately, and grew worse as we proceeded. The weather was now very cold, and I had a lively time with a helpless man in my cariole, and another, almost as helpless, behind with the baggage train. When the Indians came up to camp they helped me, but they were generally a long way in the rear.

I shall never forget a scare Mr. Woolsey gave me on that trip. It was the next morning after leaving Edmonton. We had started early in the night, and I was running behind the cariole, holding the lines by which I kept it from up- setting. We had left the others far in the rear. Mr. Woolsey was fast asleep; myself and dogs were quietly pursuing the narrow trail, fringed here by dark rows of willows. The solitude was sublime. Suddenly from the earth beneath me, as it seemed, there came, unearthly in its sound, a most terrible cry. I dropped the line and leaped over a bunch of willows, feeling my cap lifting with the upward motion of my hair. My pulse almost ceased to beat. Then it flashed upon me it was Mr. Woolsey having the "night- mare." I was vexed with myself for being so startled, and vexed with him for commit- ting so horrible a thing under such circumstances, and I have to confess it was no small shake that I gave that cariole, saying at the same time to Mr. Woolsey as he awoke, "Don't you do that again!" As he was feeling chilled I suggested that he alight and walk a bit, while I dashed on to make a fire; all of which we did, I having a big blazing fire on when Mr. Woolsey came up. I melted snow and boiled the kettle, and we had our second breakfast, though it was still a long time till daylight. The Indians did not come up at this spell, so we left some provisions beside the fire and went on. That was a very hard trip on all of us. Mr. Woolsey, wrap him as I would, seemed likely to freeze to death every little while. Smith's hand was growing worse, and he was in intense pain with it. I was in sore trouble with my passenger and my patient. Sometimes I had to roll Mr. Woolsey out of the cariole in order to get him on his feet and beside the fire. At times the condition of things was ludicrous in the extreme.

Before daylight the second morning—for we were two nights on the way—I was a long distance ahead of Billy, and was becoming anxious about him. I knew Mr. Woolsey was cold, so I stopped in the lee of a bluff of timber, and making a big fire put down some brush, and then pulled the cariole up to this, and half lifted, half rolled Mr. Woolsey out beside the fire, and finally got him on his feet. Then I turned to get the kettle, for I had taken this and the axe and some food from Bill's provision sled because he was always so far behind. Just then I smelled something burning, and there was Mr. Woolsey standing over the fire, fairly smoking. His coat sleeves were singed, and when he sat down his trousers burst asunder at the knees, and the rent almost reached from the bottom hem to the waist band.

We both laughed heartily. I could not help it, but Mr. Woolsey's "unmentionables" were certainly past mending. By-and-bye we came out upon our own provision trail, and I saw that father and party had passed on the day before; and now as we would make good time from this in to the mission, only twelve miles distant, I felt like waiting for Bill, so I said to Mr. Woolsey, "You had better walk on and warm up while I wait for our man, as the poor fellow wants all the encouragement he can get." With much bracing and lifting I got Mr. Woolsey to his feet, and expecting him to start on, busied myself with my dogs; when presently, looking up, I saw him walking out on the road to the plains. I shouted to him, "Where are you going?" And he answered back, "I am going homeward." I told him he was wrong, but he was stubborn in the thought that he was right, and I had to run after him, and fairly turn him around, and show him the track made by father and his party homewards, before I could convince him he was wrong. This was now his ninth winter in the West, and still his organ of locality was so defective that he would lose himself in a ten-acre field. Kind, noble, good man that he was, yet it was impossible for him to adapt himself to a new country. He would always be dependent on others.

When Smith did come up, I encouraged him, telling him to pluck up—only twelve miles, and a passable road at that, then home, and nursing for him. Then I dashed after Mr. Woolsey, tucked him into the cariole, and in a short time was at the top of the very steep hill opposite the mission. Here I was in another box. I dare not go down with Mr. Woolsey in the cariole, yet the dogs saw home and were eager to jump over the brow, and dash down the precipice. I held them back, and called to my passenger to get out, which he essayed to do but could not. There was a coulee on one side of the road, and a brilliant idea struck me. Deciding to bring the force of gravity to aid me in my dilemma, I upset the cariole on to the side of the coulee. Out rolled Mr. Woolsey, and he kept on rolling until he reached the bottom of the gully. This suppled him somewhat, and now, with the sides of the gully to help him, he rose to his feet. I waited to see him stand, and then, almost weak with internal mirth, for I did not want him to see me laughing, I followed my dogs over the hill and drove on to the house. After unharnessing my dogs, I went back to meet poor Billy, and help him down the hill.

Many a laugh Mr. Woolsey and I had afterwards over that trip, though at the time there were occasions when things looked serious. Poor Billy Smith had a terrible time with his hand. Inflammation set in, mortification threatened, and some of our party had to work day and night to save him. Jonas and his companion came in some hours after us, and for several days Peter and Jonas worked on the translation of some hymns into the Stoney language. Then Jonas, with such help as father and Mr. Woolsey could give him, and with a copy of these hymns in the syllabic characters in his bosom, set out on his three hundred mile tramp to his mountain home. Fortunately he missed any such mishap as that which his friends encountered on their return home, and reached his people in good time, and was able to teach others these Gospel hymns, for which he had travelled so far in the intense cold of a Northern winter.

CHAPTER XI.

Visited by the Wood Stoneys—"Muddy Bull"—A noble Indian couple—Remarkable shooting—Tom and I have our first and only disagreement—A race with loaded dog-sleds—Chased by a wounded buffalo bull—My swiftest foot-race—Building a palisade around our mission-house—Bringing in seed potatoes.

DURING the winter of 1864 a camp of about forty lodges of Wood Stoneys came to the mission from the north, and stopping with us for a couple of days, pitched across to hunt for buffalo for a while. These people frequented the wooded country to the north of the Saskatchewan, and were known as "wood hunters." Moose and elk, deer and bear, and all manner of fur-bearing animals in this country were their legitimate prey, but occasionally they made a raid on the buffalo. They were great gamblers and polygamists, and generally a pretty wild lot. They spoke the same language as the Mountain Stoneys, with some shades of difference, mostly dialectical. These people had been gone about a month across into the buffalo country, when they sent us word to come for provisions. We went, and found them in a thicket of timber, among rolling hills, near Birch Lake, south-east of the mission about seventy-five miles. From them we secured four splendid loads of dried provisions and grease; but we had a time of it in getting out of those hills with our heavily-loaded sleds—many a pull and many a lift before we came to anything like a decent road.

I want to introduce right here "The Muddy Bull," a gentleman I became acquainted with some time in January, 1864. When I say "gentleman," I mean it in its literal sense. He was one of "nature's noblemen." We came across him on one of our trips, and made arrangements with him to become our hunter. While we were hauling in meat, he and his family followed the buffalo, and he killed and hauled in and staged near his camp. Thus we lost no time in securing the meat, and very soon had a fine pile in our store-house. While we were hauling in we made his lodge our home. His wife was a natural lady, and I have often thought "Muddy Bull" and his wife gave as fine an example of married life, as it should be, as I ever saw. When I first knew these people, they were not nominal Christians, had not been married (though they had a fine family of children), had never been baptized; but for all that they were really good people.

Later on father had the pleasure of marrying them, and of baptizing and receiving them into the Church. I had no doubt about their growth in grace, for I saw this take place. But the question which often puzzled me was, "When were they converted?" for it always seemed as if they were already converted when I first met them. Noah and Barbara became their Christian names. "Muddy Bull," as I shall still call him—for at the time of which I write he was not baptized—was a splendid hunter. He had made a study of the instincts of the animals within his range. Soon after the time of our first meeting he killed seven buffaloes within fifty feet square of ground, and that with an old pot-metal flint-lock gun, muzzle loading and single barrelled at that. I have seen him with the same gun, and with his horse at full gallop over a rough country, knock three buffaloes down, one after the other, almost as fast as an ordinary hunter would with a Winchester. Then the quality of the animals spoke the true hunter. Many men could kill, but not many could pick as "Muddy Bull" could. No wonder that, having found him, we retained him as our hunter for several years.

It was while we were hauling meat home that Tom and I had our first and only disagreement. We had been bosom companions, had slept together and eaten together, had undergone all manner of hardship side by side; but one morning, before daylight, in driving out to where our loads were, Tom took offence at something, and right then and there challenged me and my dogs to race him and his dogs. I protested that we could do it anyway—I was stronger and swifter than he, and my dogs were better.

"No, sir; you must prove it," was his answer. So we arranged each to load a cow, meat and head and tripe. The animals we were after were about half a mile apart. We were to see each other load, then come out to the road at a place twelve miles from home, and at a given word race the twelve miles in.

We loaded and came out to the rendezvous arranged. There we boiled our kettle and ate our lunch in silence, then hitched up the dogs.

I said, "Tom, are you ready?" He answered, "Yes!" The next word was a simultaneous "Marse!" and off we went. My dogs were ahead. I took the road and let them go at their own pace for a couple of miles. I did not even take off my coat, but ran along behind the dogs. Presently we came to a bit of plain, perhaps a quarter of a mile long, with bush at either end. As I reached the farther end, and was about to disappear in the woods, I cast a look behind, and saw that Tom was just about emerging on the plain at the other end. I saw I was already a long way ahead, but now my blood was up, and pulling off my coat I stuck it in the head of the sled, then made a jump for a small dry poplar, and with a terrific yell broke this against a tree. My dogs bounded away as if there were no load behind them, and we went flying through the woods and across bits of prairie. All of a sudden I met a procession of old women, each with several dogs attached to *travois* following her. They had gone in to the mission with loads of provisions to cache in our store-house for use in the spring when the various camps would move in from the plains for a time. As the old ladies stood there effectually blocking the way, I shouted to them as I ran, "Grandmothers! all of you give me the road, I am running a race!" It was amusing to see the quick response of the old women. Those dogs and *travois* were pitched into the snow in short order, and as I flew past them, thanking them as I flew, I could hear the words come after me: "May you win! may you win, my grandchild!"

I was thankful that I had passed the old ladies so quickly and so easily, and could not help but speculate as to how my friend behind might find them. Reaching the big hill, I threw my load over on its side, and let it drag down like a log, then at the foot of the hill righted it up, and dashed on across the river, and up to the store-house. I then unharnessed my dogs, unloaded the sled, put away both harness and sled, went over to the house, washed and changed, and still there was no sign of my competitor.

Days after I learned from Peter that when Tom met the old women, they stood in long line, women and dogs and *travois*, as if petrified, and quietly waited for him to break a road around them, through the deep snow. This had delayed him, and also worried his dogs considerably. Tom, like many another man, had brought on the trial, and later on saw his own presumption, and was sorry for it. He and I never spoke of the race, until he was going away for good, some two months later, when he mentioned it, and asked me to forgive him. I told him I had nothing to forgive, and we parted the best of friends. I have often thought of him, and hoped he would continue to be the same manly, honorable fellow he always was while with us.

Father did not take very kindly to dog-driving, but occasionally he made a trip. "Muddy Bull" sent us word that the meat of four animals was staged at a certain place, about forty miles from the mission. Peter was busy at something else, so father took his train and went with Tom and me for the meat. We camped by the stage, had our supper, and then went to work to load our sleds. This was always careful work. There was no mere pitching things upon the dog-sled. You must load plumb and square with the centre of your narrow sled, and then lash securely, or there would be no end of trouble *en route.*

We had loaded our sleds, and all was ready for a start in the morning, when father overheard Tom and me saying that if he were not with us, we would start now.

"What is that? Don't let me hinder you, young men," said father, and hitching up, we started home, reaching there about two hours after midnight; but I think father did not feel like repeating the dose—for some time, at any rate. He was past the age when men feel capable of such work right along. However, he and Peter and I made another short trip with dog teams, across the White Mud River, in search of the white clay from which the river took its name. This clay was useful in whitening chimneys and walls, and made even a log-house look far more respectable. We found the clay deposit, and then as we tracked buffalo going northward, we concluded to camp and have a hunt. Tying up our dogs, we started out on snowshoes, each one taking a different direction. The snow was very deep. In the woods it was heavy, but on the plains, where it was better packed, one could make much faster time. Presently I heard a shot, and going to where the sound came from, I saw Peter standing at a little distance from a huge bull. The animal evidently was badly hit, and had settled himself into a bed in the deep snow. I went over to where Peter stood, and taking my snowshoes off, stuck them into the snow, and then walked up towards the head of the bull, never dreaming that the huge brute would again stand up. He was a magnificent animal, with fine horns, long shaggy beard, and very black woolly mane and neck. Thinking that he was dying, I stood admiring his beauty and powerful frame, when, without a moment's warning, he sprang at me—sprang something like the clay pigeon does when the trap is pulled—and I bounded from before him for my life. Down the slope, across a valley, up the opposite hill, I flew, nor did I even look back until I stood on the summit of the knoll. Then I saw the bull going back, and again settling himself in the same snowy bed. Gathering up my courage, I approached him more cautiously and shot him in the head, killing him instantly. When I saw my flying tracks in the snow I could hardly believe that I had made such leaps and bounds. Peter said he "never saw anything like it," and probably he never had.

"I bounded from before him for my life." (*Page 124.*)

For some time we had two men sawing out lumber at the old place beyond Smoking Lake, and at intervals we made flying trips out there for this lumber. For instance, if we reached home on Friday night, instead of starting back on Saturday to the plains, we would go out to the lumber shanty, thirty-five miles distant, and loading up, reach home with our loads of lumber the same evening. This would give us Sunday at home, which, though not happening often, was always a delight.

Now, as the spring was drawing on, and the snow beginning to melt, we rushed this lumber out, and in doing so had to travel for the most part at night, as the snow would be too soft for dogs in the day. Besides this, we took out a large number of tamarac logs, to make a strong, high picket around the mission house. Father saw that this was prudent to do, from what our experience had been in the fall, when the large camps came in around us. Then the Indians to the south, the hereditary enemies of those we were amongst, would very soon know—if they did not now know—of our settlement. Already stolen horses and scalps had been brought into the camp beside the mission, and it would follow inevitably that the avenger would come along later. A large, strong palisade would command respect from the lawless around home, and be a great help from enemies who might come from a distance.

In the meantime, Larsen and father, and in fact everybody who had an odd hour to spare, had gone on with the work on the mission house. As we had no stoves, it was thought necessary to build two immense chimneys in the house, one at each end. This took time and heavy labor. Then the drying and dressing of the lumber for floors and ceilings and partitions was tedious work, as anyone knows who ever had anything to do with "whip-sawed" lumber. You could hardly give away such boards in these days of saw-mills and planing machines, but our party had to straighten and plane and groove and tongue and bead, all by hand, and out of very poor material.

All were looking forward to the finishing of the new house, and none more than my mother. For seven months she had been obliged to put up with the crowded conditions of our comparatively small one-roomed log building. Thirteen of us called it home, ate there when we were at the mission, and nearly all slept there. All the cooking, washing, and other household work was done in this little place. Then strangers would come in for a night as they travelled to and fro. True, there were not many of these, and their coming was a welcome change, even if the house, already much crowded, became more so for the time being. Indians, too, would visit the missionary, and these must be welcomed to his home, or they would go away with a very low estimate of the faith he came to propagate; and of course upon mother came the brunt of the discomfort. No wonder she was looking ardently for the finishing of the new home.

Father worked hard—indeed all did—but there were so many things to do, so many hundreds of miles to travel, so many mouths to feed, such crude material to work with, such economy to conserve, that we could not rush things, though we seemed to be rushing them all the time.

The last trip of the season we made with dog-sled was to bring some seed potatoes from Whitefish Lake. We had deferred this on account of frost, but now were caught by heat. The snow melted before we were half way home, and we had to take poles and push behind those loads for long, weary miles before we struck the river, when we had the ice for the rest of the way home. Peter, Tom and I brought about twenty bushels between us, and by the time we got them to Victoria those potatoes were worth a great deal, for they had cost us many a push and tug and pull to get them through sound and safe.

CHAPTER XII.

Mr. Woolsey's farewell visit to Edmonton—Preparing for a trip to Fort Garry—Indians gathering into our valley—Fight between Crees and Blackfeet—The "strain of possible tragedy"—I start for Fort Garry —Joined by Ka-kake—Sabbath observance—A camp of Saulteaux—An excited Indian—I dilate on the numbers and resources of the white man—We pass Duck Lake—A bear hunt—" Loaded for b'ar "—A contest in athletics — Whip-poor-wills — Pancakes and maple syrup—Pass the site of Birtle—My first and only difference with Ka-kake.

EARLY in April I took Mr. Woolsey and my sister Georgina to Edmonton. Mr. Woolsey expected to return east during the summer, and was to make his farewell visit. My sister was invited by the Chief Factor's lady, Mrs. Christie, to spend some time with her. We travelled on horseback with pack-horses. We were three days on the trip up, and I was two coming home, after safely delivering my passengers at Edmonton.

Soon after I came back father startled me by saying he wanted me to go to Fort Garry to bring out the supplies for the two missions,

Whitefish Lake and Victoria. He said that the Hudson's Bay Company had notified all missionaries that their transport was needed for their own business, and suggested that the missionaries make their own arrangements for obtaining supplies. Therefore he wanted me to go down and purchase and bring up what was needed for the Methodist missions on the Saskatchewan. I was to take horses and men from both missions, and also purchase some cattle down there to bring up for work and for dairy purposes. Thus I found my work cut out for me for several months ahead, and I immediately commenced making preparations.

The Indians had now begun to come in in large bands, and very soon our valley was full of life. Men, both wild and partially civilized, surrounded the place, though a large number of the former, instead of coming in with the camp, had gone the other way, seeking for scalps and horses, and, if successful, would be drifting in later on. Already that spring there had been a big fight between a party from our camp and the Blackfeet. The Crees were surrounded and kept for two nights and nearly two days in the pits they had dug with their knives. The Blackfeet were ten times their number, and kept them well under cover, but did not muster courage sufficient to rush in, or the Crees would have been cleaned out in short order. As it was, several were killed. Of two I knew, one was killed and the other shot in the breast, but recovered as by a miracle.

Father and Peter would now be on a continuous strain of work for the next six weeks, planting, hoeing, teaching, preaching, healing, counselling, civilizing and Christianizing. Night and day, constant watchfulness and care would be required. A very little thing might make a very big row. Life and death were in the balance, and the missionary had to be a man of fine tact and quick judgment as well as a man of prayer. The turbulent element was sometimes in the majority, for large numbers of Plain Crees had come in with the quieter Wood Indians. Saucy, proud, arrogant, lawless fellows they were, every one of them, yet, withal, courteous and kind if one only took them the right way; and to be able to do this we were studying all the time.

Mother and my young sisters moved in and out among these painted and war-bedizened crowds, all unconscious of their danger, and it was well it was so; but father and myself, and others also, felt the strain of possible tragedy. Maskepetoon when at the mission was a tower of strength, and a great source of comfort; but there were a number of jealous factions even in his own camp, and born chief that he was, he often found them very hard to control. This was the first attempt by any Church to establish a mission among these people, and under such circumstances, we put our trust in Providence—but kept our powder dry.

It was with an anxious yet sanguine mind that, during the last days of April, 1864, I left parents and mission party behind and started eastward for Fort Garry. I had with me a French half-breed, Baptiste by name, and we were to be joined by the men and horses from Mr. Steinhauer's mission some fifty or sixty miles farther east. We had a pack-horse to carry our food and bedding, and were in the saddle ourselves—that is, we had two Indian pads, as the Mexican saddle had not yet made its appearance so far north.

The second day we were joined by our comrades from Whitefish Lake, my friend Ka-kake being one of the number. They had a cart with them. Our party now was complete, and consisted of five men and fifteen horses. As it was early in the season, and our horses had come through a pretty hard winter with considerable work, and consequently were somewhat run down, we travelled slowly, averaging about thirty miles per day. Our provision was pemmican, but we supplemented this as we travelled with ducks, geese, and chickens. Yet, notwithstanding all our efforts to procure variety of diet, many a meal was hard grease pemmican straight.

We travelled only the six days, faithfully and rigidly observing the Sabbath, which told in the manifest improvement in the condition of our stock. We had prayer morning and night, my men taking turn in conducting worship. On Sunday we rested and sang a number of hymns, and as we were speaking Cree all the time, I was constantly improving myself in the language, and learning the idioms and traditions of the people amongst whom it would seem my lot was to be cast.

We passed Fort Pitt, and continuing down the north side came to Jackfish Lake, where we found the camp of Salteaux that frequented this lake feasting on the carcases of a great herd of buffalo that had been drowned in the lake the previous winter. Too many had got together in some stampede across the ice and had broken through and were drowned; and now that the ice was off the lake, the carcases were drifting ashore. These improvident people were glad to get the meat. They offered us some, and though Ka-kake took it out of deference to their kindness, he watched his opportunity and threw it away. Some of the younger men came to our camp that night, and as Ka-kake was a sort of kinsman of theirs, he undertook to show them the folly of their course in some lawless acts which they were charged with perpetrating (for these fellows had a hard name). One of them, after listening to Ka-kake's talk, began to speak quite excitedly, and said: "You seem to make much ado about our taking some plunder and demanding tribute of parties passing through our country. What will you think when we really do something, for we are disposed to organize and take these Hudson's Bay forts, and drive all the white men out of this country; then you will have something to talk about!"

Just here I thought it was my turn to join in the conversation, and quietly snatching a handful of blades of grass, I picked the shortest and smallest one of these and held it in my other hand, then looking at the excited Indian I said: "My friend, I have listened to you; now listen to me. Look at this handful of grass in my hand: These are many and big and strong, and this little one in my other hand is small and weak and alone. This little weak, lone grass represents the white man as he now is in this country. There are a few traders and a few missionaries, but they are as this little grass in strength and number, as you look at them; but if you hurt them in any wise, as you say you will, this bunch of many and strong grasses I hold in my hand represents the multitude your own conduct would bring into this country to avenge them. You say you can easily wipe out the white men now in this country—have you thought that they have the guns and the ammunition and the real strength? Can you or any of your people make guns or ammunition? Then why talk so foolishly and thoughtlessly?"

Ka-kake in his own way strongly endorsed what I said. Then I began to tell those fellows something about civilization and the numbers and resources of the white man, and they opened their eyes at what I had to say. I wound up by telling them that though the white man was so numerous and strong, yet he did not want to take their country from them by force; but when the time came the Government would treat with the Indians for their country and their rights; that the missionaries were in the country sent by the "good white men" to prepare the Indians for a peaceful transition into a better condition than they now were in. "For instance," said I, "you people had plenty of buffalo near you last winter, and now you are living on rotten, drowned meat, and yet you are men. There is something wrong, and if you will only listen, and put away evil thoughts and bad talk, such as you gave us just now, we will show you something better." All of which Ka-kake strongly corroborated, and when the Salteaux went away he turned to me and thanked me for the way I had spoken to that man and his party. Said he, "It will do them good; they will think about it." At the same time we tethered our horses and guarded them well.

Crossing the North Saskatchewan at Carlton by means of a small skiff and swimming our horses over, then passing Duck Lake, where I had hunted ducks two years before, and which, twenty years hence, was to become the scene of the first real outbreak, under Riel, in 1885, we crossed the south branch, where Batoche some years later settled and gave his name to the place. The next day we had a bear hunt, but did not get the bear, as the brush was too dense, and we had no dog. We killed several antelope, and (it seemed to me) ate them up in no time.

Crossing the alkali plains we journeyed through the Touchwood Hills. Here we had another bear hunt, and this time Ka-kake killed the bear, and we put him, great big fellow that he was, into our cart to take him on to camp. Then followed a lively time with the hitherto very quiet old horse that was pulling the cart, for suddenly he seemed to find out what he was hauling, and attempted to run away. Failing in that he then tried to kick the cart to pieces, and in many ways showed his objections to the load. He might, if he had travelled in the East, have heard the phrase, "being loaded for b'ar," but if he had, he most emphatically drew the distinction between that and being loaded *with* bear. However, we got him to camp at last, and very carefully took him out of the shafts before we let him see the bear. Thus antelope steak and bear's ribs, with fowl occasionally, and eggs of more or less ancient date now and then, varied the monotony of the everlasting pemmican.

We caught up to a party from Lac-la-biche going the same way. They were French half-breeds on their way into Red River with their furs. We found them first-rate travelling companions, and fully enjoyed their company. At one of our evening encampments, one party challenged the other to a contest in athletic sports, and we beat them badly, my man Baptiste leaving their best man easily in a footrace. He said to me, " Mr. John, I will run fust; if he leave me, then you will run." " All right, Baptiste," said I; but there was no need for my running, as Baptiste won the race for us. Of this I was very glad, for he also was a French mixed blood, and of themselves. Then, in jumping and throwing the stone we were far ahead, and my men were greatly pleased at our victory. I confess to feeling well pleased myself, for I delighted in these things at that time.

Continuing our journey, we left these people to come on more slowly. We crossed Pheasant Plains and the Cut Arm Creek, and camped one evening on the high bank of the Qu'Appelle River, beside a spring. In the evening shade, as we were sitting beside our camp-fire, suddenly I heard a cry which thrilled through my whole being: "Whip-poor-will!" "Whip-poor-will!" came echoing through the woods and up the valley, and in a moment I was among the scenes of my childhood, paddling a birch canoe along the shores of the great lakes, rioting among the beech and maple woods of old Ontario. For years I had not heard a whip-poor-will, and now the once familiar sounds brought with them a feeling of home-sickness.

The next afternoon Ka-kake and I, leaving our companions to cross the Assiniboine above the mouth of the Qu'Appelle, detoured by way of Fort Ellice, and here also I had another memorable experience. Mrs. MacKay, the wife of the gentleman in charge of the Fort, very kindly invited me to have supper with them. As we would have plenty of time to rejoin our party afterwards, I gladly accepted, and what should be on the table but pancakes and maple syrup! I had not tasted maple syrup for four years, had not had a slice of bread for two years, had not even tasted anything cooked from flour for some time. No wonder I can never forget those cakes and syrup! Verily the memory of them is still sweet to my taste. Not that I am an epicure—by no means—but these were things I had been accustomed to, almost bred on, all my life previous to coming to the North-West.

We rejoined our companions at Bird Tail Creek, camping on the spot where now the town of Birtle stands. This was Saturday night, and during that Sunday camp on the bank of Bird Tail Creek I had my first and only difference with Ka-kake. Some hunters on the way out by Fort Ellice camped beside us, and from these Ka-kake learned that friends of his were camped about twenty miles farther on. About the middle of the afternoon, he and the two Indians from Whitefish Lake began to catch their horses, and make as if they were going to start. I asked what they meant, and Ka-kake told me that they were going on, and would wait for us in the morning. I said he might go on if he chose, but I would not consent to his taking the horses belonging to Mr. Steinhauer, as these were in my charge, and I did not intend to have them travel on Sunday. He was firm, but I was firmer; and finally Ka-kake turned the horses loose and gave it up.

I do not think I would be so hard now that more than thirty years intervene and my outlook is broader, and my thought more liberal; nevertheless, I believed I was right at the time, and therefore acted as I did.

CHAPTER XIII.

Fall in with a party of "plain hunters"—Marvellous resources of this great country—A "hunting breed"—Astounding ignorance—Visit a Church of England mission—Have my first square meal of bread and butter in two years—Archdeacon Cochrane—Unexpected sympathy with rebellion and slavery — Through the White Horse Plains—Baptiste's recklessness and its punishment—Reach our destination—Present my letter of introduction to Governor McTavish—Purchasing supplies—"Hudson's Bay blankets"—Old Fort Garry, St. Boniface, Winnipeg, St. John's, Kildonan—A "degenerate" Scot—An eloquent Indian preacher—Baptiste succumbs to his old enemy—Prepare for our return journey.

THE next day Baptiste and I went ahead. We were now three-quarters of the way down, our horses had picked up well, and I wanted to hurry on so as to get through my business as quickly as possible, and give more time to the homeward trip, when we would have heavy loads. The first night we camped with a large party of plain hunters, on their way out for a summer hunt. These men were from all over the Red River settlement, from the White Horse plains, and Portage la Prairie. Their encampment was like a good-sized village. They must have had five hundred or more carts, besides many waggons. Then this number would be very much augmented from Fort Ellice and other points eastward.

Looking on one of these parties, and remembering that two such parties went out on the plains after buffalo every summer for the purpose of making dried provision; that some of these would make fall and winter forays for fresh meat; that this same thing was going on in the Saskatchewan country among the same class of people, and that from Texas to the North Saskatchewan many Indian tribes were living on the buffalo, winter and summer;—I say, that if one thought of all this, he would begin to have some small conception of the extent and numbers of the buffalo. Moreover, if he continued to think, he would wake up to the appreciation of a country that could in its crude and wilderness condition maintain such countless and enormous supplies of food, and that of the choicest kind.

These were the men who owned the rich portions of Manitoba, the Portage plains, and the banks of the Assiniboine and Red Rivers; but what cared they for rich homesteads so long as buffalo could be found within five or six hundred miles? These owners of the best wheat fields in the world very often started out to the plains and were willing to take their chance of a very risky mode of life, forsooth, because they came of a hunting breed, and "blood is thicker than water," and environment stamps itself deep upon the race. In going through the camps, eager as I was for eastern news, I could find none. What signified it to these men that the greatest of civil wars was then raging on the continent beside them? What thought they, or what did they know of the fact that they were on the eve of a great national and political change, and that the old life would soon have to give way to a new order of things? Their teachers either had not sought to enlighten them, or had failed to make them comprehend, if they did desire to do so. No wonder that in their ignorance they were led astray in 1869-70, and again in 1885. They could talk about horses and buffalo, and battle with the Sioux and Blackfeet, and count their beads and mutter prayers, but apparently were sublimely ignorant of all things else. Alas! that this should have been the case, for these men were and are full of fine traits of character. Kind, hospitable, chivalrous, brave, I have ever found them. Surely scores of years of preaching should have done something better for them.

We jogged along, Baptiste and I, across the

Little Saskatchewan, and by the two crossings of the White Mud, and coming to the third crossing in the evening, found a Church of England mission with the Rev. Mr. George in charge. Mrs. George was very kind, and for the first time in two years I had a square meal of bread and butter. Oh! how good it was! I had to fairly curb my appetite. Next morning Mrs. George gave us a fresh loaf of bread and some butter for our lunch that day. But do you think we could wait until noon? We had not gone a mile from her hospitable home when I said, "Baptiste, don't you think we could carry that bread and butter somewhere else very much better than on that pack-horse?" "Oh, yes, Mr. John," was his expressive answer. We thereupon alighted, took the tempting loaf from the pack, ate it with eager relish, and then went on quite satisfied.

We rode through the Portage, finding at that time but two white men settled there. As I had a letter for Archdeacon Cochrane, we called for a few minutes on that venerable prelate. I found him quite an old man. That day he seemed somewhat discouraged, for he asked me if I did not think these people (meaning the mixed bloods among whom he was laboring) must first be civilized before they could be Christianized. I ventured to say that I thought

Christianity was the main factor in real civilization. Then he asked me what my opinion was of the war in the States, and I told him that I knew very little about it, and had seen very few papers—none whatever for some months. Then he said he was in sympathy with the South. At this I was astonished, but did not venture to say anything, for he was an old man, and I but a boy. I wondered as I rode away how a gentleman of his age and experience and education and calling could hold such views as to be in sympathy with rebellion and slavery. There must be something in this I do not understand, thought I. But if there was any good reason for such a position I have never yet come across it.

That night we camped with a brother-in-law of Peter's, living at the High Bluff, who received us kindly. The next day, continuing our journey, we jogged along the north bank of the Assiniboine, around the Big Bend, and through the White Horse Plains. As we were passing a house Baptiste said, " Mr. John, my friends used to live here; stop a minute and let me see." So we approached the house and found that the woman of this place was Baptiste's cousin, and though many years had elapsed since they had met, the recognition was mutual and joyous. As the day was extremely warm, this woman offered us some nice cold milk, of which I, remembering I had not had any for some years, drank very sparingly, but my man Baptiste indulged in it recklessly.

Mounting our horses, we resumed the chronic jog, and had not gone many miles when I heard a groan, and looking back, saw Baptiste with his hand pressing his stomach, and looking woefully dismal.

"What is the matter?" I enquired.

"Oh! Mr. John, I am sore," was the woeful answer.

"I thought so," said I. "You should not have drunk so much milk; you deserve to be sore."

In the evening we came to the farm of Mr. Gowler, to whom I had letters from both father and Mr. Woolsey, and whose home I hoped to make my headquarters while doing my business and gathering my stock and loads for the West. Riding into the yard, we found the old farmer had just finished churning, and was enjoying a bowl of fresh buttermilk. He kindly offered me some. I declined with thanks, but said my man was very fond of milk. Mr. Gowler at once gave him a big bowl of it, and Baptiste dare not refuse. His code of etiquette would not allow him to decline, and, though in misery, he nevertheless drank it.

Like many another simple person, he was the slave of social rule.

Mr. Gowler had come out in the Hudson's Bay Company's service, by way of Hudson's Bay. In due time he had gone free, and settled on the Assiniboine, a few miles west of Fort Garry, and at this time had the largest farm in the Red River settlement. He was an English Wesleyan Methodist in the Old Country, and though he had allied himself to the Anglican Church when he came out here, yet he retained a warm feeling toward those of his early persuasion. Thus Mr. Woolsey and father had met him, and thus I had come to him to arrange for a camp, a pasture and a home while in the settlement, all of which Mr. Gowler heartily welcomed me to, and in such a way that I was at home at once. The next day I rode in to the Fort, and presented my letters of introduction and credit to Governor McTavish, who said he would help me in any way he could, inviting me at the same time to take my meals, when in the vicinity, with him and his officers. I also became acquainted with his nephew, John McTavish, who was at that time Chief Accountant, and who rendered me many kindnesses during my stay in the settlement.

I had no trouble about the year's supplies for the missions, as these had all been requisitioned for, as usual, early in the year. My business was the arranging of transport. I must secure carts and harness and oxen, and, as the several plain-hunting parties had recently started out, I had some difficulty in finding enough for my needs. But after some days' hunting around, I secured all I wanted; had bought my oxen, fine big fellows, paying on an average £7 (about $35) apiece; also four quiet milch cows, for which I paid from $15 to $18 each, thinking as I bought them how much they would be welcomed by our people at yonder mission. I also bought ten sacks of flour, paying £1 12s. per sack of ninety-six pounds, and 2s. for the sack. Add to this the freight to Victoria, and the first cost there of each sack would be $18.50. I gave five sacks to each mission, which, allowing a sack for the men of each party *en route*, would give the missions four sacks of flour for the year. This would be a wonderful advance on any previous experience in the bread line at either of those places. I bought, too, a promising colt, descendant of "Fire Away," a very famous horse the Hudson's Bay Company had imported from the Old Country. For this three-year-old colt I paid £14, or $70 of our money. I handled, in making my purchases, the first "Hudson's Bay blankets" I had ever seen. These were large

5s. and £5 notes, issued by the Company, and which I drew from them on father's order.

In the course of my business I was in Old Fort Garry a number of times. I saw St. Boniface, then a very small place, just across the river, and the home of Bishop Tache. I was in and out of the five or six houses which then formed the nucleus of the little village called Winnipeg. I rode frequently through the parish of St. John's, passing the house of Bishop Anderson, the Anglican head of Rupert's Land. I went down into Kildonan and spent a night in the home of the Rev. Dr. Black, who was one of father's dear friends. I also met there the Rev. Mr. Nisbet, who later on founded the mission work at Prince Albert. I visited some of the original Scotch settlers, and was looked upon by the elders as a degenerate, because, as they expressed it, "She couldna spoket the Gaelic." I spent two Sundays in this settlement, hearing Dr. Black the first Sunday, and remember thinking that his fine Gospel sermon was "broad" in more senses than one. The next Sabbath I worshipped with the Anglicans, and heard the Rev. Henry Cochrane preach an eloquent and inspiring sermon, and was glad that a genuine native had reached such a position. I have often felt sorry that the men who were instrumental in raising him to this height of development did not themselves keep ahead sufficiently in example, as well as in precept, but by their failure caused their weaker brother to offend, and later on to fall terribly from his high estate.

It has taken many centuries of progressive development to give a very small percentage of the stronger races of men the will power and ability to understand and observe the meaning of the word temperance. It is a very small sacrifice (if it may be called such), yet an essential factor with missionaries in their work with the pagan races, that they themselves be through and through transparent and consistent, or else to these will come the greater condemnation. But, not to further moralize, I will go back to the loading of my carts and the gathering of my stock, preparatory to my journey westward.

My man Baptiste had found his old associates and whiskey too much for him, and forgetting wife and children on the Saskatchewan, had disappeared. I could not give the time to looking for him, but hired instead one of Mr. Gowler's sons, Oliver by name, and as I was still short of help, was very glad that I came across a gentleman by the name of Connor, and his son, a young man about my age, who were desirous of making the trip to the Saskatchewan. As they had but one cart between them, I secured the son to drive carts for me. My party was also joined by a Scotchman who was desirous of crossing the mountains to British Columbia, and who, finding that we were starting westward, asked permission to travel with us. He also had but one cart. When we started, as the Whitefish Lake party had horses pulling their carts and would travel faster (especially in hot weather) than we could, I let them go on ahead of us. Our party was composed of Mr. Connor and the Scotchman, my two men and myself—five in all.

CHAPTER XIV.

We start for home—A stubborn cow—Difficulties of transport—Indignant travellers—Novel method of breaking a horse—Secure provisions at Fort Ellice—Lose one of our cows—I turn detective—Dried meat and fresh cream as a delicacy.

I THINK it was about the last of June or the first of July that we rolled out of Mr. Gowler's farmyard on the trail leading across the plains. The first day or two we had considerable trouble with our cattle. One cow was determined to go back, so I caught her and tied her behind a cart to which was attached a ponderous ox. She rebelled at this, and threw herself down, but the ox kept on as if the weight dragging behind was a small matter. Coming to a shallow creek in which there were some sharp stones on the bottom, the cow, finding the action of being dragged over these too much, jumped to her feet, and after that led on as we wished. Very soon all broke in to the routine of the journey in good shape, and we had very little trouble after the first week with any of our loose stock.

Let one of those ironless carts squeak, and the cows were up and alongside with all the alacrity of a soldier answering the bugle note.

There had been considerable rain, and for the first three weeks after we started it rained very heavily at times. As there was not a tent in the party, we each got under a cart, and while the rain came perpendicularly we were passably dry; but the mosquitoes were sometimes awfully annoying. The copious rains made the roads very heavy in places, but we came along as far as the second crossing of the White Mud without having to move loads. Here we were forced to raft everything, which means a long delay, as also a great amount of labor. I made a raft of cart wheels, and pulling this to and fro with ropes we ferried our goods and chattels over. Having let the Indians go on, my party as now constituted was altogether "tenderfoot" in its make up, though with me my two years on the Saskatchewan modified this. As it was, I had all the planning and also a large portion of the work to do. To unload your carts and make your rafts, and ferry over by piecemeal your loads and harness and cart-boxes and whole travelling outfit; to watch your stock in the meantime, and that closely, or else lose hours or even days in hunting for them; to keep your stuff from the wet from above as well as beneath, and in doing so get more or less wet yourself; to make smudges to save your cattle and horses from being eaten alive by "bull-dogs"* and mosquitoes; to fight these exceedingly energetic denizens of the air the while you are trying to do this work I have just enumerated,—I say that if you have ever been, or ever will be, in such a case, you will have an idea of summer transport across bridgeless and ferryless streams in a new country.

Having passed the second, we went on to the third crossing of the "White Mud," and like the man with the two daughters whom he called Kate and Duplicate, we simply duplicated the last crossing here, only that it was "the same and more of it." The creeks had been very small on our way down, but now seeing them so full after the heavy rains, and giving us so much trouble to cross, I began to apprehend some difficulty at the Little Saskatchewan, for this was a river, and rapid at that. However, we stopped short of this one morning for breakfast, and while the boys were making a fire I walked on to the river, and was delighted to note that while it was muddy and swift, it was still fordable. This I knew without trying, as I had

---

* A name given to a species of black fly common on the prairies, and significant of their ferocity and persistency in attack.

taken its measure on my way down. Just then, as I stood for a moment on its bank before returning to my camp, two travellers on horseback, with a pack-horse, came down the hill on the other side. They looked at the stream, and at once pronounced it unfordable; then, without stopping to ask me, got off their horses, and unsaddling and unpacking, took out their axe and went for some timber to make a raft. I thought I would have some fun with them, so waited until they had carried up some logs for the raft. Then as they stood on the bank resting for a little, I walked down into the stream and across to them. As I had estimated at first glance, there was no more than twenty or twenty-four inches of water. These travellers looked astonished, and seemed indignant that I had not told them. "Why did you not tell us the river was fordable?" said one. "Why did you not ask me?" I answered. Then one blamed the other who was acting as guide, and told him he ought to have known better than to let them make such fools of themselves. Here I spoke up and said, "Well, as it is fordable, you had better saddle up and come across and have some breakfast with us." But right here my reader will note the difference in men. One takes notice of the country he passes through, and hopes to recognize it when next he comes this

"I headed her out again into the lake." (*Page 155.*)

way; another says he knows it all, and acts as this guide did.

Fording the Little Saskatchewan, we continued our journey. One day we stopped for noon on the shore of Shoal Lake, and here while our stock were resting I made an experiment. We had brought with us from the mission a fine strong mare about seven years of age, which had never been broken to either drive or ride, and was very wild. She would follow the carts and stay with our horses, that was all. My plan was to take her out into the lake and break her there. We made a corral with the carts, and I lassoed the mare, and haltering her, stripped off my clothes and swam out into the lake with her, then quietly slipped on her back. She gave a plunge or two, but only succeeded in ducking herself, and then settled down to straight swimming. After a while I headed her for the shore, but as soon as she got squarely on the bottom she began to buck, so I headed her out again into the lake, and presently I could take her out on the beach and canter up and down as nicely as with an old saddle-horse. Then I dressed, and putting a saddle-pad on, rode her all the afternoon. Rolling on as well as we could, heeding but little the mud and mosquitoes and pelting rains, in good time we reached the Assiniboine. We were two days rafting that stream, and the large part of another in doubling and portaging up the big sand hill which forms the north bank of the Assiniboine at this point.

Leaving my party in camp on the bank of the Qu'Appelle, I forded this stream and rode over to Fort Ellice, hoping to secure some dried meat or pemmican, as we were living now entirely on flour and milk, and I wanted to use the flour as little as possible. On my way through the woods which thickly covered the hill between the Qu'Appelle and Fort Ellice, I met four white men on foot, carrying new flint-lock guns. The guns and their appearance branded them as belonging to the Hudson's Bay Company, and being "green hands," as all the newly received employees were called, I enquired of them where they were going. One of them answered, "The Lord knows, for we don't." My next question was, "What are you looking for?" and they answered in chorus, "Our supper." "Why," said I, "are there no provisions in the Fort?" "None," they answered; "we were given these guns and some shot and powder, and told to hunt for our suppers." This was poor encouragement for me in my quest for provisions. I had noticed that the leader, while he had a new gun on his shoulder, did not have any flint in the dog-head. "Well, my friend," I said, "you will never kill your supper with that gun you carry." "Why," he asked, "what is the matter?" I pointed out to him what the matter was, and then all began to look at their guns, and I went on, for about the most dangerous place you can be in is where a number of tenderfeet are handling guns.

I confess I was disappointed about the provisions, and felt that it would be too bad to have to use up the little flour I was taking home, for it was three hundred miles to the next Fort on our way. However, being young and of a sanguine turn of mind, I galloped on to the Fort, and again called on Mrs. McKay, who corroborated what the men said, telling me that the Fort was in sore straits for food; but that she expected soon to hear from Mr. McKay, who had gone on to the plains. Fortunately for me, while we were talking a party drove into the Fort with several cart-loads of provisions, and thus I secured both pemmican and dried meat, and those poor "green hands" did not go supperless to bed that night. My two men and I went breadless to bed instead, and for many subsequent nights also, for I was determined to save the flour for mother and the others at home.

Steadily we pushed our way westward, some days, when cool and cloudy, making good time, then, when it was hot, going more leisurely.

Travelling early and late, we would keep at the long trail. Then an axle would break, and this would bring us up standing. Sometimes a dowel-pin snapped, or a felloe split, and mending and lashing still we rolled toward the setting sun. Once we lost one of our cows, and I had to retrace our way some miles in looking for her. The country we were passing through was dotted with dense brush, and as the "bull-dogs" were bad, the cow had gone into a clump of trees to rid herself, if possible, of her enemies, whose name truly was legion. Now, to gallop back farther on the trail would in all probability be futile in finding the cow. So I went to work on the detective plan, and first sought for a clue. This I got from Oliver and Jim, my men, who were positive as to when they had seen the cow last. So I went back on one side of the road, carefully watching for the track, and coming to the spot where the boys had seen the truant last, I then crossed the road, and keenly looked for a track on the back trail, but found none. I was now pretty sure that the cow was between me and the carts, and on the other side of the road from that I had come on. So, keeping a little way out from the road, I followed up the carts, and by-and-bye came to the track of the cow. She had turned out from the trail and gone into a thicket, and I had to leave my horse at its edge to follow her track into it; but keeping on the trail, I at last found her, almost enveloped in the foliage, and in the shadiest spot she could find.

The next morning, while the others were supping their tea or drinking the new milk, I took some dried meat, and with this skimmed and ate the cream on the milk in the pail I had hung under the cart the night before. Dried meat and fresh cream might not be a "dainty dish" for an epicure, but then one must not forget the exquisite relish we had around us in our perfect freedom of out-door life; in our solid beds, wet or dry, on the bosom of "mother earth," under the carts; the pure atmosphere, the beautiful sunrise and sunset, the lovely undulating, park-like country we were travelling through, giving us constant change of scene; the many gems of lakes and lakelets we skirted, the superb health we generally enjoyed—each and all of these were the best of tonics, and under such conditions even hard grease pemmican was good.

CHAPTER XV.

Personnel of our party—My little rat terrier has a novel experience—An Indian horse-thief's visit by night—I shoot and wound him—An exciting chase—Saved by the vigilance of my rat terrier—We reach the South Branch of the Saskatchewan—A rushing torrent—A small skin canoe our only means of transport—Mr. Connor's fears of drowning—Get our goods over.

WE HAVE now been nearly a month on the way, and are becoming well acquainted with each other, for there is no better place than around the camp-fire, and on a trip like ours, to size up men and display one's own idiosyncrasies. Mr. Connor, the gentleman who had joined me at the Red River, proves to be a very good companion. He has travelled and read; was at one time, in the early forties, a minister of the Methodist Church, but owing to some misunderstanding had given up the ministry and gone afloat—and is still floating. He is generally bright and cheerful, and very helpful, but sometimes falls into a streak of melancholy, which, after all, darkens his own day more than that of any one else. He drives his own cart. This he has shingled with pieces of tarred bale covers, and at night sleeps in it. His yoke of steers, though at first somewhat balky in mud-holes, after I have drilled them a few times, and got them to recognize my voice in a real western yell, come along all right. His son James, who is one of my men, is a short, sturdy fellow, and being strong and hearty, is fast adapting himself to this new life. My other man, Oliver, is but an over-grown boy; has had very little opportunity in life, no chance at school, and is rather simple-minded, but willing and strong. The Scotchman, who is on his way across the mountains, walks by his own cart and horse most of the day's march, and is "canny and carefu'" about the camp; for the most part silent and reserved, but in a pinch, and at river crossings, lends a strong hand. Such a journey as we are on is new to all but myself, and I, though all my life on the frontier, am but in my fourth year in this the greater West.

We had three dogs with us, one belonging to the Scotchman, and the others to me. Both of mine were a present from a clergyman I met in the settlement, one a duck dog, and the other a small rat terrier. The latter supported the two former on the road by killing gophers for them,

This little fellow was extremely agile. He would jump up on my foot in the stirrup, and at the next leap be in the saddle beside me. There he would rest for a little while, perhaps until the next gopher popped in sight, when with a bound he would be away; and this he would keep up the whole day long. At night I might wrap my blanket as tightly as I pleased about me; the little scamp would crawl in somehow and sleep in my bosom. One day when we were hunting moulting ducks during our noon spell, he got after a big stock duck, and taking hold of the tail feathers of the bird, the latter made for the lake with the dog in tow. The little fellow was gritty and held on while the duck towed him far out into the lake. It was highly amusing to see the small dog being whirled along by the duck, who was flapping his featherless wings and swimming at a great rate. Presently the dog, wanting to bark, opened his mouth, and the duck dove under immediately it was loose. My little pet swam ashore after affording us no little amusement by his unusual adventure.

One Saturday evening we camped in the Touchwood Hills, and found ourselves in the vicinity of a solitary lodge occupied by an old Indian and his aged wife. They told us that their children and people had gone out on the plains. The report was that the buffalo were not far away, and they were hoping to hear from their friends before long. The *mesas-koo-tom*, or service berry, were very plentiful all through the hills, and this old couple had gathered and dried a large quantity. I was glad to trade a bag of these from them to take home to our people, for any kind of dried fruit had been a scarce article with us.

On Sunday afternoon two boys came in from the plains with a horse-load of dried provisions. They were the old man's grandchildren, and had come for the old folks. The boys said the buffalo were a good day's journey south of us, which would be about fifty miles. Monday morning I traded some dried provisions from the old man, and we parted company.

I think it was the fourth day afterwards that we camped in a small round prairie, backed by a range of hills and fringed around by willow and poplar brush. We had pulled our carts into a line, with our camp-fire in the centre. We were sufficiently north, as we thought, to be comparatively safe from horse-thieves and war parties, so we merely hobbled our horses, and making a good smudge near our own fire, we rolled in our blankets, each man under a cart, except Mr. Connor, who slept in his. Some time in the night I was awakened by my little dog, who had crept under my blanket as usual, and now startled me by springing forth and barking vigorously. As I raised myself on elbow, I saw that the two larger dogs were charging at something quite near. The moon was about three parts full, and the night quiet and almost clear. From under the shadow of the cart I could see our horses feeding near the smoke. Presently I discovered an object crawling up to come between the carts and the horses. At first I thought it was a big grey wolf, but as the dogs rushed at it, I saw that it did not recede, but came on. I reached for my gun and watched closely, and presently saw the object pick up a stick and throw it at the dogs. This convinced me that it was someone trying to steal our horses. His object evidently was to creep in between us and our stock, and gently driving them away, he would then cut the hobbles and run them off.

Having made sure that what I saw was a human being, and a would-be horse-thief, or worse, I immediately planned to intercept him. So I in turn began to crawl along the shade of the carts until I was under the last one, which was Mr. Connor's. Here I waited and watched until, seeing the fellow repeatedly frighten the dogs away, I was sure it was a man. He was slowly coming up on hands and knees, and was

"I took deliberate aim, and fired at him." (*Page 165.*)

now near the first horse, when I took deliberate aim and fired at him. My gun was loaded with shot, and fortunately for him was only a single barrel, or I would have given him the other, for I was not at that moment in a mood to spare a horse-thief. My shot at once knocked him flat. When the smoke had cleared away I saw him starting to crawl off, so I jumped for him, on which he rose to his feet and ran for all he was worth towards the nearest brush. I dropped my gun and picked up a pole that lay in my way, and was overtaking him fast when he reached the thicket; then thinking he might not be alone, I ran back for my gun. My companions by this time were all up, and we made ready for an attack. Tying up our horses, we watched and guarded until daylight, but were not further molested.

By this time I concluded that the thief was alone, and I became very anxious about him. I knew I had hit him, but to what extent I did not know; so taking a man with me, we went on his track and found that he had lost considerable blood, had rested and, we supposed, had in some way bound up his wound and then gone on. As we tracked him I concluded by his step that he was but slightly hurt, and would reach his camp all right. This relieved my mind considerably, but it was not until the next year we heard about the fellow. Then it came out that I blew the top off the man's shoulder, and after a hard journey back to camp, he lay some three months before recovering. Having ample opportunity for reflection, he saw the error of his former way and vowed to steal no more.

This Indian had heard from the old man and his two grandchildren, whom we left in the Touchwood Hills, that a small party of white men had travelled west, having with them some good horses. He concluded that this would be a "soft snap," and acted accordingly. Had it not been for my vigilant little rat terrier, he would have taken our horses and left us in a pretty fix. I have always felt thankful I did not kill the fellow, but most certainly I wanted to at the time. If my gun had been loaded with ball, or that bit of prairie had been longer—for I was coming up on him fast, and the pole I carried was a strong one—the results might have been different.

We were now approaching the South Branch of the Saskatchewan. The streams we had crossed thus far were as child's play compared to this. It was midsummer, and the snow and ice in yonder mountains, six or seven hundred miles away, would be melting, and the mighty river be a swollen torrent. Would we find a boat there or not? If not, how were we to cross? These were thoughts and questions which kept coming up in my mind all the time. It is very easy under some conditions to say to another man, "Do not cross the river until you come to it," but when you know the river to be big and wide, and the current like that of a mill-race; when you know that there is not a man in your party as good even as yourself in such a case; when you feel all the responsibility of life and property, involving the well-being of many others, you cannot help but worry.

We were still several miles from the river, when I galloped ahead to find out the best or the worst that might be in store for us. Coming to the river I saw it was booming. Great trees and rafts of driftwood were being swept down by its swishing currents, and with a strain of anxiety I rode down the several hills to the river's brink, and felt almost sick at heart when I found there was no boat in sight. Very often the Hudson's Bay Company kept a boat at this point, but now, search as I would, there was none to be found, and I rode back up the hill with a heavy heart. However, at the top of the hill I now discerned a pole stuck in the ground, and thought I saw something white at the end of it. Galloping over, I found a note tied to the pole, which said, "Down in the woods in the direction this stick points, there is a skin canoe."

This had been arranged by the Company people at Carlton for the benefit of Mr. Hardisty, whom they expected to be on his way west from an eastern visit. They had not a boat to spare, so they made this small skin canoe, brought it here and left it staged up in the trees for his use when he should come along. The note also said, "In the bow of the canoe you will find a chunk of hard grease." This was to pitch its seams with and make it waterproof if possible. Now for a light travelling party, with saddle and pack-horses, this would be sufficient, but for a heavily loaded train like ours it seemed like a "small hook to hang your hat on." But even this was something, and I soon went to the spot in the woods indicated and found the canoe placed high on the limbs, to keep it from the wolves and coyotes, who would soon gnaw its skin covering. I saw it was very small, being made of two buffalo cowhides, stretched over a frame of willows, and in it were two paddles and a parcel, which undoubtedly contained the grease.

It was late Saturday evening when we camped upon the shore, and my companions were almost paralyzed by the appearance of the river. It was fortunate that they had all day Sunday to become somewhat familiar with the sight of this mad current and its tremendous volume of water. Monday morning I was up with the day, and calling my two men we boiled the kettle, chopped some chunks from our mass of pemmican, and sat down to breakfast. Presently Mr. Connor crawled out of his cart, and sitting on its edge, said "Good-morning." I invited him to a cup of tea and a piece of pemmican, but to my astonishment he very solemnly said, "Before I do anything to-day I want to come to an agreement with you men as to how long you are prepared to stay here and search for the body of anyone of us who may be drowned here to-day." It was very early in the morning, and myself and men were not very hungry—at any rate, the one dish of uncooked pemmican was not very appetizing—but when the above very anti-tonic remarks fell in sombre tones from the venerable-looking man's lips, I noticed that Oliver dropped his pemmican, while his eyes widened and his face blanched. I saw that I must do something, or else I would not be able to take Oliver near the river that day. So I laughed out a regular "Ha, ha!" at the old man's strange demand. "It is no laughing matter," said he. "Yes it is—a very laughable matter," I answered, "that a man of your age and experience should make such a proposition, for in the first place we do not expect anyone to be drowned here to-day, and more, if any of us should drown in that current, what would be the use of searching for the body? If I am the one to be drowned, don't you lose a minute looking for my body, but go on taking the stuff across, and take it to its destination; but my word for it, we will get across all right. Come along and have a cup of tea." This he did without saying any more about drowning, and he worked like a trooper all the rest of the day, helping in any way he could. Some years later Mr. Connor was drowned, and he may have felt premonitions of his coming fate that morning.

Breakfast over, we immediately began operations. The first thing was to carry the canoe to the water's edge, then taking the grease, and biting off a mouthful, chew this until it became like gum; then with finger cover over the seams wherever they occurred in the canoe. When this was done we launched the canoe, and for the first trip put in about three hundred pounds, as this, we thought, with the two men necessary to work her, might be all she could carry. Then we had to track or trail our canoe up the river a long way, for the current would carry us down a great distance while crossing. This we did by one pulling on a line and the other wading along the shore and keeping the canoe out from the rocks; then when we did let go, the two in the canoe had to paddle as hard as they could, for the rough hide and flat shape of the clumsy thing made it very heavy in the water. Having reached the other side, and unloaded and carried up our goods out of the reach of a possible rise of water, we had to again pull our canoe a long way up the river on that side, in order to reach anywhere near where our stuff was in crossing again. After the first trip we found that we could average about four hundred pounds with the two men, and keeping hard at it the long summer's day, drying our boat while we lunched or dined or supped, and ever and anon repitching it with the grease, we had most of our stuff across by sundown, and were once more in camp—and no one drowned!

CHAPTER XVI.

A raft of carts—The raft swept away—Succeed in recovering it—Getting our stock over—The emotionless Scot unbends—Our horses wander away—Track them up—Arrive at Carlton—Crossing the North Saskatchewan—Homes for the millions—Fall in with father and Peter—Am sent home for fresh horses—An exhilarating gallop—Home again.

THE next morning we pulled our carts as far up the river as there was beach to move on, and then, crossing over several times, got the remainder of our freight, harness and camping outfit across. In the meantime we were making a raft of the carts. We took the wheels off and fastened them to the boxes, then tied the whole together, and as I purchased a long rope in the settlement, my plan was to fasten one end of this to the raft and carefully coiling up the rest, take a third man into the canoe to pay it out while we would paddle for the shore as fast as possible. Arrived there, we would jump out, and with the rope gently warp our raft to the shore. But that current was strong and treacherous, and when we, after a fearful

"We went at a furious rate on that swirling, seething, boiling torrent." (*Page 173.*)

struggle, did succeed in jumping ashore, to my dismay at the first strain the rope broke, and away with the rush of current went our raft of carts.

There was just one spot, about a mile down, where we could land those carts. If we missed that the current would sweep them to the other side of the river, and on into a series of rapids below. To jump into the canoe, to chase that raft, to hitch to it, and then to paddle for the shore as we went at a furious rate on that swirling, seething, boiling torrent was our instant action. How we worked! How I watched that one spot where it was possible for us to land! How I calculated the time when I would pay out line, and once more try to warp our raft in! How as by a miracle we did make the one spot, and held our raft, and, securing it, sat down on the shore and rested, and were thankful!

But our difficulties were not yet all mastered. At a glance I saw we had heavy work before us to take those carts out of the spot where we landed. A steep, almost perpendicular bank, covered with brush, must be climbed at the outset, and then a road of some two or three miles made in order to reach the spot where our goods were. Though I saw all this, yet as I lay there with the carts on the home side of the river at my feet, I felt profoundly thankful.

The first thing to be done was to take the carts out of the water and put them together, then, by wading and tracking and pulling and pushing, to take the heavy skin canoe up stream, and again cross, as our stock were still on the south side. Here came the tug of war, for those cattle were afraid of the wide stream and the strong current. We drove them up and started them in at the spot where the flow of water struck for the other side, but all in vain; they kept coming back on us. We shouted and waded in after them. Many times we gave them a fresh send-off. Finally we towed one over after the canoe, and rushed the balance in after this one, but they went back on us again. We took another, and still the rest would not follow; but we gave them no peace, and finally, after hours of the hardest kind of work, they struck out and swam across, some of them going a long distance down stream. Eventually all crossed, and at a late hour on Tuesday evening we were camped—goods and carts and stock and men—on the north side of the South Branch, and as yet no one drowned!

To say we were thankful is to say but little. Why, even the seemingly emotionless Scot of our party unbent that evening and became quite funny. But we also were very tired, and to add to this, in my case, the soles of my feet were badly cut with the sharp stones, and the fine sand had got into the wounds, causing me intense pain. The next morning my feet were badly swollen, and only with great difficulty could I put them to the ground, so I depended on Oliver and Jim to hunt up the stock. After being hours away they returned and reported the most of our horses lost. There was no other resource but to soak my swollen feet and moccasins in the river, and start out to look for them. By taking a big circle from the river, I finally found their track, and running or walking or crawling, as occasion required, I followed them up, my progress depending on the nature of the soil and the grass. Sometimes I was obliged to go on my hands and knees, in order to detect the faint tracks left by those unshod horses.

After hours of such tracking and of closest scanning of the track, I came to the summit of a hill, and was exceedingly fortunate in catching a glimpse of my horses disappearing over the brow of a hill in the distance. My seeing them as I did saved me hours of tracking, and enabled me to catch up on them fast, for I did not stop my race until I reached the spot where they had disappeared from view. Then, as they were not in sight, I began my tracking again, and very soon came to the truant sin a swamp.

I caught one, and jumping on bare-back, made those horses fairly fly back to the river, where I was gladly welcomed by my companions, who had become anxious at my long absence.

Working on into the night that evening, we succeeded in climbing the hill, and camped about three miles from the river. The next day we reached Carlton and the North Saskatchewan. Here we had a wider river to cross, but were fortunate in securing the loan of a boat which, although it was old and very leaky, yet enabled us to cross a cart and its load at each trip. Our cattle, too, did not give us so much trouble as at the South Branch. We were not quite two days in crossing. Here we had a long, high hill to double up with our loads, but finally were on the top of it, and on the home side of the two big Saskatchewans. I was a very glad man in consequence. The hundreds of miles yet to travel, the many smaller rivers and streams yet to cross, seemed as nothing to what we had passed; and we were all pleased that the backbone of the trip was now broken.

Two years before this, father and I had ridden up this hill on our first trip to the plains. No change had taken place since then. Here were the thousands of homesteads and countless acres of rich grass and soil, verily homes for the millions; but as yet the units of men were not here, doubtless because there was a Providence in all this, and the time had not come for settlement.

The same afternoon that we left the north side of the river, I came across an Indian who took a strong fancy to the horse I was riding, the one I had broken in in the lake, and which, though a fine animal, had caused me a deal of trouble, and had no doubt taken the lead in going so far a few days before. As the Indian had a stout grey horse which he said was good in the harness, we agreed to "swap even;" so, dismounting, we changed our saddles from one horse to the other, and each went his own way satisfied. My grey pony proved himself first-class in the cart.

Early and late we rolled westward, across wide valleys and over great ranges of hills, from whose summits we looked out upon magnificent stretches of country, which made my companions, beholding it for the first time, open their eyes and exclaim in wonder at the wealth of soil and great variety of scenery on every hand.

Travelling for days we reached and passed the rendezvous of the threatening Jackfish Lake Indians, and I was glad to note that there were no fresh tracks in the vicinity. They were either out on the plains after buffalo or in the north hunting moose. As we had a very small party I had felt anxious about these people and was thankful for their absence. However, the next day our number was strengthened by unexpectedly meeting father and Peter. Father had come to Fort Pitt on missionary work, and in doing so had met Ka-kake, who had told him that I could not be very many days behind; so he had come on, and thus we met, which was a source of profound satisfaction to me. Father and Peter were a host in themselves, and as we were now geting farther into the country where tribal war was rife and war parties from the south frequent, to have our little party so handsomely reinforced was a comfort and joy to us.

Father was pleased with my purchases of cattle, and complimented me on the condition of the stock all round. He thought we could now afford to push them, as they would have plenty of time to fatten for winter after we reached the mission. From daylight until dark, therefore, stopping only to feed, we kept at it and made good time. The old landmarks of the bridle-path across the continent—Red Deer Hill, Frenchman's Butte, Fort Pitt, Two Hills, Moose Creek, the Dog Rump, Egg Lake—each in turn was left behind.

Camping on the home side of the latter one evening, father said to me, "John, you may gallop on to the mission in the morning and see your mother and sisters; and if you can find them, bring us some fresh horses." We were now about fifty miles or more from the new mission, and had reached the limit of wheel-tracks on the north side of the Saskatchewan, so that our party would have to make the trail the rest of the way through a new country with more or less bush.

Early the next morning found me astride of my little sorrel—the one the Indians had named "The Scarred Thigh," because he had once been tossed by a mad buffalo—and away we went on the steady jump. After a time, thinking I might be riding my horse too fast, looking at my watch I said to the sorrel, "We will trot for half an hour, and canter the other half;" but though I tried this several times, we would invariably be on the dead canter before the thirty minutes for trotting had nearly expired. So finally, as the little sorrel seemed ready for it and eager to go, I let him out. What a gallop we had that day! Soon we were past Saddle Lake, and had reached the summit of the Snake Hill. Every spot near the trail was now familiar to me, for I had walked and ran, and pulled and pushed, and frozen and starved between Saddle Lake and Victoria; but on this occasion my whole being was thrilled with the pleasant anticipation of seeing my loved ones. Possessed of a profound sense of gratitude for the mercies of the long trip now so nearly over; with a strong, springy, willing horse under me, a clear sky above, lovely landscapes on every hand, every foot of soil under my horse's feet full of great possibilities, an exhilarating atmosphere striking my face, filling my nostrils, inflating my lungs at every jump, it is no wonder that morning's ride is indelibly impressed on my memory. I thoroughly enjoyed it; and so far as I knew this was righteous joy, which methinks will live forever. I had a bit of dried meat with me, which I ate as I rode. About ten o'clock I stopped to grass my horse. Throwing the saddle down I turned him loose at the end of my lariat, and tying the end of this to my arm, flung myself on the grass and slept.

If I had not been so much of a tenderfoot as I still was, I would not have fastened my horse to myself, for in doing so I was running great risks of being killed. Of this, however, I did not then think, but slept on, and presently waking with a start, saddled up and started into a lope once more. When fairly under way, looking at my watch, I saw we had not spent a full half hour at our resting and feeding-place. Then I apologized to the sorrel, but he kept on the steady canter all the same, and before noon we were at the mission, joyfully welcomed by mother and friends. Fifty miles before dinner, and both horse and rider as ready for work as ever, and I may be pardoned in saying "that was a horse, and this was a man."

CHAPTER XVII.

Improvements about home—Mr. Woolsey's departure—A zealous and self-sacrificing missionary—A travelling college—I feel a twinge of melancholy—A lesson in the luxury of happiness—Forest and prairie fire—Father's visit to the Mountain Stoneys—Indians gathering about our mission—Complications feared.

PART of that afternoon I spent at home with mother, and during part of it hunted up our horses, and finding them, corralled them for the night. I noted the new house was finished and that mother was comfortably settled once more in a substantial home. True, it was without any furniture or stoves, but Larsen was hard at work at the former, and time and money would eventually bring the latter. (Mother, of all women I know, is most strongly possessed of patience and sublime resignation to the lot of the wife of a pioneer missionary.) I saw, also, that the stockade around the mission-house was finished; that another field had been fenced, broken and planted; that the prospect of a garden crop was good, and that our chance of barley for soup next winter was largely within the possibilities. I saw, too, a number of garden patches that the Indians had fenced in, hoed and planted with the small share of seeds the mission could give them. With most of these aborigines, this was the very first effort to till the land. In short, I saw that those at home had been at work, and that things were beginning to look like permanent occupancy.

I missed the genial, kindly presence of my old friend, Mr. Woolsey. He had returned to Ontario, following the route down the river in one of the Hudson's Bay Company's boats, and thus I had failed to meet him. Nine years on the Saskatchewan, from 1855 to 1864, in Hudson's Bay fort, in Indian lodge, beside many a camp-fire, he had preached the living gospel of a loving Saviour. In doing this work he had undergone untold hardships, always and everywhere handicapped by physical infirmities. Transplanted from the city of London, Eng., into the wildness and wilderness of the far west; having had no experience or knowledge of the conditions of frontier life in a new country; with no knowledge of the language of the Indians—indeed, I venture to say he had seldom seen an Indian—in the presence of the physical difficulties which were as legion everywhere around him in his new field, he was altogether dependent on those around him. This, too, in a country where the horseman and the hunter, and the man ready in resource under every or all of the exigencies of real pioneer life on the frontier, were tried to the utmost. If upon such men as these there was the constant strain and burden of difficulty and great hardship, what must have been the experience of Mr. Woolsey, arriving there fresh from the comforts of English life.

For nearly a decade this devoted servant of God had journeyed incessantly up and down through the length and breadth of the Upper Saskatchewan and among the foot-hills of the Rockies. He had alternately shivered and sweltered, starved and feasted. When freezing he was given a camp-fire in the frozen snow and colder air to thaw him. When scalding in the burning heat of the long midsummer day on the treeless plains, he had to refresh him a cup of tepid swamp water, in which any ordinary sight might behold extraordinary life. When starving, even he, notwithstanding his strong Sabbatarianism, was forced to travel on in quest of food.

One cold winter day, he and his French half-breed guide and dog-driver were within a hard day's travel of the Rocky Mountain Fort. It was Sunday. They had food neither for dogs nor men. Mr. Woolsey would fain have kept the Sabbath, and gone hungry in so doing, but

REV. THOMAS WOOLSEY.

(From a photograph taken soon after his return from the North-West.)

his materialistic guide and driver hitched up his dogs, and making ready, said: "Well, Mr. Woolsey, you stop here and pray; I will go to the Fort and eat." Mr. Woolsey then allowed himself to be wrapped in the cariole and taken to the Fort, where he could both eat and pray.

When he feasted, he might sup and dine and breakfast for days on fish, another time on rabbits, another period on eggs, in all the various stages of incubation; for change he would pass from eggs to moulting ducks, and for days these would be his diet. Then would come the longer intervals of buffalo diet. Tongues and marrow-bones, and back fats and bosses both little and big, and dried meat and pemmican, either straight or disguised in *rush-o* or *rab-āboo*, just as you please. Ah! then he was feasting indeed when he had buffalo meat. It is true at times there would come to him the strong craving of a true Englishman for slices of bread and butter, or chunks of plum pudding, or even a potato; but what was the use, my friend would heroically away with such longings, and content himself with his hard grease pemmican.

He mastered the Syllabic system so that he could read and write in it, and also teach to others the use of this wonderful invention which God gave to James Evans. It was curious to listen to him reading a chapter in the Cree Testament to a group of Indians, himself not understanding ten words in the chapter, while his hearers were intelligently grasping every word. Scores are now in heaven whom he taught to read the words of the blessed Master. Under a blanket-covered tripod on the plains, at the foot of a tree in the woods, in the shade of a skin lodge, by the glare of a camp-fire, or in his little room at a Hudson's Bay Company's Fort, he held school, and the graduates in syllabic learning of his travelling college are scattered all through this western country to-day.

He gained a smattering of the Cree, so as to make himself understood at a pinch. For instance, he and Susa, Samson's brother, were once camped in the woods near Pigeon Lake. When retiring for the night, Mr. Woolsey wanted to arrange an early start next morning, and spoke thus: "Susa, *ke-yah ne-yah wa-buh-ke we-butch a-wass*," (You me to-morrow soon get out); and Susa understood, and acted accordingly.

Like my father, Mr. Woolsey never presumed on a knowledge of the language, never gave the shortest or simplest kind of an address or sermon without an interpreter, never made the too frequent mistake of attempting to speak of sacred and important matters in an unknown tongue. He was considerable of a medicine man, too, and many a poor Indian was relieved and aided by his hearty help in this way. Among the Hudson's Bay Company's employees he had quite a name as a kind physician.

I have been Mr. Woolsey's interpreter, guide, and general "roust-about," his confidante and friend, for the past two years, and now he has gone into a far country; and as I look upon the valley, the scene of our association under strange and sometimes exciting circumstances, I feel a twinge of melancholy. But here are mother, and sisters four, and little brother, and the evening passes quickly as we recount to each other the experiences of the summer.

The next day I started back with some fresh horses, and met our party coming along famously. For picking a road Peter is a genius, and all hands worked willingly in chopping out the road, brushing swamps, and bridging creeks. Late in the evening of the next day we rolled down the hill into the beautiful valley of the Saskatchewan at Victoria, ours the first carts to ascend the north side of that great river so far west as this point. Slowly the star of empire was moving in the line of destiny.

Fifty-six travelling days from Fort Garry—stock all right, carts sound, goods dry, and twenty-five pounds of flour still left in the bag we began on when we left the Red River settlements—such was our record, and father was pleased; and because he was pleased I was happy. I took the flour in to mother, and she and the children and Larsen luxuriated in hot rolls for supper. We unloaded the four sacks I had brought with me, and everybody felt good, for this seemed to us a great quantity at the time; though really, for our large party, taking into consideration, too, the fact that our house was the only one for miles, and that the Hudson's Bay Company officers and men, and brother missionaries, as well as occasional travellers and fur traders, stopped with us as they passed to and fro; that sometimes we had from five hundred to fifteen hundred Indians beside us, and more or less coming and going all the time, with many sick among these,—I say, when one thought of all this, the item of four hundred and nine pounds of flour for twelve months did not seem much. It was, however, the first time in the history of the place and vast surrounding country that so much breadstuff had been stored. Why, when you arithmetically calculated it, there was actually one and one-quarter pounds per day! No wonder mother saw a Christmas pudding, and no end of cake for the many sick folks to whom she so much delighted to minister. No wonder my sisters laughed, and the little baby brother gleefully shouted, "Cake! plenty cake!" If some of the pampered among men in centres of civilization, jaded with the *ennui* of plenty, had visited that lone mission on the evening of our arrival, they would have learned a lesson in the luxury of happiness that comes from contentment with little.

The cows I had bought were also a great source of comfort to our party. These assured us of milk and butter, and if other resources failed, of beef also. Of those who came with me from Red River, the Scotchman traded his cart and harness to father, and packing his horse went on to Edmonton, thence taking the trail through the Yellowhead Pass for British Columbia, never to be heard of by us since; Mr. Connor and his son concluded to winter beside us, and went to work putting up a shanty to live in. Thus our small English-speaking company was augmented by two more, for which we were very thankful.

One mishap had come upon us during my absence, in the burning of our saw-pit and saws, together with considerable lumber, by a forest and prairie fire which came in from the south "like the wolf on the fold." This was quite a set-back, as the getting out of lumber by hand is slow work.

I found that father and Mr. Steinhauer, with Peter, had made a long trip among the Mountain Stoneys. Our visit of the last fall had resulted in bringing about half of these down country, as far as the upper crossing of Battle River. There father and party met them, and spending a few days with that camp, continued their journey, and found the rest of these " sons of the mountains and foot hills " in a valley some forty miles north of where our mission at Morley now is. Father was full of this visit to the Stoneys. Their hearty reception of the missionaries, their earnest and joyous listening to the teachings of the Gospel, their appearance and demeanor, had won his ardent sympathy. Then the country they lived in—lovely valleys, springs of water, beautiful hills, and in the background immense ranges of majestic mountains—father declared the whole country was one great revelation to him of Canada's rich heritage in this vast North-West. He said he would do what he could to urge upon the Mission Board the need of establishing a mission among these mountain people.

Having more stock necessitated the making of more hay and providing more stable room; then we went to work at replacing the timber and lumber which had been burnt, for our purpose now was to build a church as soon as possible.

The large one-roomed shanty we had lived in the previous winter was our place of worship in the meantime, and when the weather permitted and the Indians were in from the plains, some central spot out on the prairie was chosen for open-air meetings. With the advance of autumn our Indian friends began to gather in to the mission. Maskepetoon's following of Wood Crees, or "mountain men," as they were called by the other Indians, were followed by many of the Plain Crees, and for days the riverbanks and crossing in front of the mission-house were alive with humanities, in all stages of growth. Horses there were in many hundreds, of all colors and grades, and dogs, it would seem, by the thousand. Shoutings and neighings and howlings incessant broke the quiet of our valley, while the smoke of myriad lodges hung over the scene.

During the summer a number of skirmishes had taken place between the Crees and the Blackfeet. Scalps had been taken home and rejoiced over by both contending camps. Warriors had gone straight from the field of blood to the "Big Sand Hills," as the Blackfoot would say, or to the "Happier Spirit Land," and many a young fellow who had no horse last spring now rejoices in the ownership of a little band, the successful stealing of which gives him a place among men. These camps have been coming into the mission, while at the same time several parties have left the south to look for horses and scalps. As these return (if they ever do) they will follow straight into the mission, which will in time complicate us, and bring retaliatory measures to our very door; but as this is the condition of the times, we must take our chance, all the while laboring and praying for a better order of things.

CHAPTER XVIII.

Maskepetoon — Council gatherings — Maskepetoon's childhood—"Royal born by right Divine"—A father's advice—An Indian philosopher—Maskepetoon as "Peace Chief"—Forgives his father's murderer—Arrival of Rev. R. T. Rundle—Stephen and Joseph — Stephen's eloquent harangue — Joseph's hunting exploits—Types of the shouting Methodist and the High Church ritualist.

BOTH father and mother have taken a strong liking to Maskepetoon, and have given the old gentleman a room in the new house, of which he is very proud. In this room he leaves his paper and books and clothes, and into it he often goes to read his Bible. His manly, courteous and kindly behavior makes it pleasant to have him in the house, and in every good work he is as the missionary's right hand. It is well it is so, for at this time the missionary needs all the help he can secure. This strange, promiscuous, turbulent crowd need careful handling. Men who have quarreled about a horse or a woman bring the case to the missionary to settle. Women whose husbands have, as they say, "thrown them away," come to him to reinstate them in their husband's favor and lodge. Widows who have been robbed by their late husband's relatives pour their complaints into his ear, and look to him to adjust their claims. Monogamy *versus* polygamy is a burning question, and very often the preacher is sorely puzzled to know what to do in the matter. All the sick in camp expect the praying man to help them. What with meetings all through the week and almost all day Sunday, father and Peter are constantly employed. Then comes the solemn gathering of the big Council, when the long-stemmed pipe is passed around, and every rite and ceremony religiously observed.

It has often seemed to me that superstition and ritualism are synonymous in the minds and lives of men. Here were these most superstitious of beings, and in all their life intense ritualism had full sway. These council gatherings, however, were fine opportunities for the missionary, who, if in the vicinity, and if he had the confidence of the people, was always invited to be present. At these would assemble both friends and foes. Conjurers and medicine men were there, who felt their craft was in danger; warriors and horse-thieves, too, who loved their life of wild lawlessness, and readily foresaw that if this new faith should have sway their present mode of life would cease. Others there were who intensely hated the white man. His cupidity, sensuality and generally aggressive conduct had at some time in their history insulted and wronged their whole being, and now they fairly loathed the sight of the white portion of the race. On the other hand were the few who had embraced the new faith, and who were in hearty sympathy with the mission.

War, peace, trade, the present, the future, their old faiths, the new one brought in by these missionaries, all these matters would be discussed at the councils, and the tactful exponent of Gospel teaching would watch his chance, and from the speeches and arguments of his audience turn the trend of thought to Christianity and civilization.

It was fortunate that at this time our mission had a strong friend and ally such as Maskepetoon proved himself to be. With consummate tact he would preside over these council gatherings, and in every one of them score a point or more in favor of the missionary and the cause he represented.

Tennyson says:

> " Here and there a cotter's babe is royal born
> By right Divine."

I will say an Indian's babe was "royal born by right Divine," when the child who became this man Maskepetoon was born: his birthright the common heritage of natural man, his birthplace the Rocky Mountains, his cradle lullaby the crash of tumbling avalanches and the roarings of mighty "chinooks." The shrill cry of the mountain lion, the deep bass note of the buffalo, the ripplings of limpid streams and the ragings of mountain torrents in their wild race to a common level—these with the pagan's death wail, the rattle of the conjurer's drum, and the warrior's shout of triumph were sounds familiar to his baby ears.

His childhood was passed in travellings constant and perilous. Winter or summer, his people had "no abiding place." He was always in the presence of the giant forces of Mother Nature. His youthful eye could ever and anon look out from some foot-hill height upon scenes which the varying shades of heaven's light so glorified that these became as pictures painted by the hand of God Himself. His young manhood was passed in those times when the rich premiums of life, love, respect, gratitude were lavishly bestowed upon the perfect horseman, the successful hunter, and the brave and victorious warrior.

Maskepetoon had a free hand in all this, and brought to himself and people great glory. As was the manner of the period, he was a polygamist, and an inveterate hater of his tribal enemies. This he had drunk in with his mother's milk, and yet as he grew into strong manhood I can readily believe this unique man had his moments of longing for better things. The Divine would stir within him so strongly at times that the crusting of centuries of sin and darkness would crack, and the man would aspire and look and long for something that he instinctively knew would be infinitely better than his present.

It is related of Maskepetoon that after he had become renowned as a victorious warrior, and already the Blackfeet tribes had given him the name of Mon-e-guh-ba-now (the Young Chief), his aged father said to him, "My son, you are making a great mistake. The glory you are now seeking will be short-lived. Delighting in war, taking pleasure in the spilling of man's blood, is all wrong. If you want to be a great man, if you want to be remembered long, turn about and work for peace. This is the only thing that will give you true fame."

Six different times did this heathen philosopher thus address his beloved son, and this proud and haughty youthful chieftain would fold his arms around his head, and bowing himself sit in silent reverence and meekly listen; but his warlike spirit would rebel against this sage advice. Yet his father's words troubled him so that at last he filled a pipe and went over to the lodge of another aged man, who was said to be wise beyond the wisdom of other men, and lighting the pipe he handed it to the old man, and asked for counsel as to what was best in life, and what was evil and should be shunned.

The humble-minded old Indian said, "Your father is more capable of advising you than I am;" but Maskepetoon persisted in seeking counsel, and then the aged philosopher cut eight small sticks of different lengths, and stood them in the ground four in a row. "Now," said this unschooled professor of ethical teaching, "these sticks represent two lines of life. I will give them names. These four are falsehood, dishonesty, hatred of fellowmen, war; those are truth, honesty, love of fellowmen, peace. I will speak of each one; and now since you have come to me, my son, I want you to open your ears and treasure in your heart what I have to say." Then in his own natural eloquence the aged man discoursed to his intent listener, and when finished he gathered the line of sticks ending in war, and said: "Shall we keep these, or shall I burn them?" "Burn them," came from the stern lips of the strong-willed young man. "Shall I bind these others ending in peace together, and give them to you in remembrance of what I have told you?" "Bind them well and give them to me," replied Maskepetoon, and thus he forsook war and became the champion of peace, and in this way became the forerunner of the Gospel of Peace which in a few years was to be preached for the first time in this new land.

In the meantime Maskepetoon's reformation was put to severe tests by the murder of his friends and fellow tribesmen, and by the frequent stealing of his horses; but he stood firm. Then came the killing of his father by the Blackfeet, and while both friends and foes, knowing him as they did, watched and wondered, still, like the mountains under whose shade he was born, he was immovable, and remained loyal to his new position as the apostle of peace in this lawless country.

It was soon after this that Maskepetoon placed himself upon record before all men as the "Peace Chief," and it happened in this wise. He and his people were encamped near the Peace Hills, close to where the little town of Wetaskewin now stands, when a large party of Blackfeet and their allies came in on their way to trade at Fort Edmonton. Under such circumstances the Blackfeet were only too glad to ask for a temporary peace, and this being arranged, they came into the Cree camp, seemingly forgetful that they had with them the very man who had killed Maskepetoon's father. Somehow this came out, and caused consternation in the minds of both parties. Said they, "If the young chief hears this, then there will be terrible war." But our hero did find out that the man who had killed his parent was in his camp. When he heard it he sent for his best horse, had him saddled and accoutred as for war, fastened him at his tent-door, and while intense anxiety prevailed, and all were nerved up for the struggle which they thought inevitable, Maskepetoon sent for his father's murderer. The man, an elderly warrior, came as to his death, and Maskepetoon waved him to a seat near himself in the tent. Passing him his own adorned chief's clothes, made of leather, decorated with beads and quills and fringed with human hair, he said to him, "Put those on." "Now," thought the frightened yet stolid murderer, "he is only dressing me out for my death," and brave men on both sides held their breath as they looked on, calmly making ready for the desperate struggle they believed was coming. Again Maskepetoon spoke: "You deprived me of my father, and there was a time when I would have gloried in taking your life and in drinking your blood, but that is past. What makes you pale? You need not fear; I will not kill you. You must now be to me as a father; wear my clothes, ride my horse, and tell your people when you go back to your camp this is the way Mon-e-guh-ba-now takes revenge."

Then the old Blackfoot found speech and said, "You have killed me, my son. You are a great man. Never in the history of my people has such as this you have done been known. My people and all men will hear of this and say, 'The young chief is brave and strong and good; he stands alone.'"

With this men breathed freely again, and women laughed for joy, and little children began to play once more among the lodges. No wonder that such a man was looking for something better than the old faith. But who was to reveal this better something to him? Thus far the white men he had met gave him no help. The trader's ambition, it would seem, reached no higher than muskrats and beaver, while the transient stay of the roystering, licentious, sporting aristocrat or eastern grandee, with his impudent assumption of superior make, did the Indian and white men who followed him great harm. But now in the fulness of time the same England that had sent to this new land rum and many a sample of spurious civilization, was sending a messenger of another type. The

English Wesleyan Conference sent the Rev. R. T. Rundle to labor amongst the Indians of the Hudson's Bay Territory. His objective point was the Saskatchewan country, and presently it was rumored in the camps that a man who talked to "Him" (meaning the Deity) had arrived in the upper country.

"Who is this mysterious being who talks with God?" "What are the limits of his power?" "What is his purpose in coming to this part of the country?" were questions frequently asked, and around many a camp-fire and in many a leather lodge this strange being was discussed. None was more curious and anxious than Maskepetoon, who finally saw Mr. Rundle at the Rocky Mountain House. Then the missionary visited his camp, which was at that time near Burnt Lake, a short distance west of where the Industrial School on the Red Deer now is.

Old Chiniquay, one of our chiefs at Morley, who was brought up in Maskepetoon's camp, tells me that from that first visit of the preacher of this new faith there was a marked change in the conduct of the chief. Later on he learned the Syllabic system, taught him by Mr. Harriott, an officer of the Hudson's Bay Company, who was stationed for some time at the Mountain Fort. Then he became a student of the New Testament, translated by Steinhauer and Sinclair into a dialect of his mother tongue, and from that day took sides with the Gospel and became the true friend of the missionary.

Two other friends of the pioneer preacher of the Gospel were Stephen and Joseph his son, whom I have already referred to in earlier chapters. The old man had been a mighty hunter. Grizzly bears, mountain lions, and all manner of game, big and little, had been his common prey, and of his pluck in battle there could be no question. With his left arm broken near the shoulder, he caught up the swinging limb, and gripping the sleeve of his leather shirt with his teeth, he charged the enemy, and in the defence of his camp did such heroic deeds with his one arm that his foes gave way, believing him to be possessed of "Spirit power."

I will never forget the old hero's eloquent harangue before a council of excited warriors, who had been discussing the desirability of driving the white people out of the Saskatchewan country. Many had been the grunts of approval and assent, as one after another wrought upon the assembly in the endeavor to stir up strife. Then old Stephen got up, and leaning on his staff, spoke as follows: "Young men, your words have made me sad. I have said to myself, while I listened to you, These men do not think. Has it never come to your minds that this big country we live in is almost empty of men, that one can travel many nights between the dwellings and tents of men, and not see a human being; and do you think this can continue? Were not these broad plains and great hills, this good soil and rich grass, and these many trees made to be used for the good of the great Father's children? I think so. I am not selfish enough to believe that all this big land was for me and my people only. No, I seem to see great multitudes occupying where I have roamed alone. Young men, the change is near, and the Great Spirit has sent his servants to prepare us for its coming. Again, young men, your words are foolish, for you are not able to drive the white man out, nor yet keep him back from coming into this country. Can you "—(and here the old man's eye flashed, and his almost palsied arm took on fresh life, pointing to the mighty river flowing near)— "can you dam that river? Can you send those strong waters back up on the mountains from whence they came? No, you cannot do this; likewise you cannot keep the white men out of this land. Can you stop yonder sun from rising in the morning? Come, gather yourselves, make yourselves strong, stop him if you can! No; neither can you stop the incoming multitudes. It will be; it must be; it is destiny. Then, young men, be wise, and listen to those who can prepare you for these changes which are coming, surely coming."

Ah, thought I, this man has attended the school of the prophets; the Infinite has spoken to him. And other men, notwithstanding the paint and feathers, and the centuries of war and ignorance, thought so too. Joseph also, like his father, was solidly on the side of the mission, and no other man I have ever been associated with lived so strictly and consistently as did this man. The law of God was to him supreme. He followed the letter as well as the spirit. The snow might be deep, the cold intense, the distance we had travelled for the day long, the way difficult; but if it was Saturday night, Joseph would work until midnight cutting and packing in wood, so that our supply would not need replenishing before midnight Sunday night. Legalism, you say. Never mind, this man was of the true Puritan stock, and his pedigree, is it not written in heaven?

Joseph also was a mighty hunter. He told me (and this was fully corroborated by his contemporaries) that quite early in his career as a hunter he had kept count of his killing grizzlies up to forty-two, then he had lost count, but had killed a large number since that time. Think of this, you Nimrods who go afield with your big bores and modern repeating rifles! Joseph's best weapon was a pot-metal flintlock, single-barrel, and muzzle-loading at that. With such a gun it required pure pluck to tackle the big grizzlies of the mountains, but my old friend was full of it. There was another fine fellow, "The Red Bank," or, as he was baptized, Thomas Woolsey, a kind, cheerful, everyday Christian, one it did you good to meet, and from whose camp I always came away refreshed and made stronger in the faith.

These men were some of the fruits of missionary labor. Rundle and Woolsey and Steinhauer had not visited distant camps and undergone all manner of hardship and risk without accomplishing good. These men I have mentioned and others, both men and women, were now the nucleus of a church, and the comfort and help of the new mission. Moreover, there were among the conservative pagans some good fellows, kindly disposed to all men, and these, too, became the friends of the mission party. There was the "Blood" man, whom I have already spoken of, who had to whoop every little while or else lose his soul, as he thought. He would have made a first-class shouting Methodist or Salvation Army man. I should not forget old Mah-mus, who could neither eat nor smoke without first ringing a small bell he constantly carried with him. He was an A1 ritualist, and would have done credit to an extremely High Church establishment.

CHAPTER XIX.

Muh-ka-chees, or "the Fox"—An Indian "dude"—A strange story—How the Fox was transformed—Mr. The-Camp-is-Moving as a magician.

"MUH-KA-CHEES," or "the Fox," was another particular friend of ours, but one who clung to his old faith. He was quite a wag in his way and created a hearty laugh around our camp-fire by describing an imaginary scene, in which he was to have settled down beside the mission and gone into farming and stock-raising, but the crowd around us would go on in the old way, hunting and trapping. He would become wealthy, adopt the white man's mode of life, dress, etc. This would go on, and one day it would be reported that the York boats with their crews were coming up the river from their long and slavish trip to the Coast, the men in harness and working like beasts of burden as they were. He would drop his work for a bit, and dress up in a neat cut coat and white shirt, and with hat cocked on one side just a little, and tobacco rolled like a stick in his mouth, with cane in hand, he would walk down to the river bank, and as the boats came up he would carelessly look over at his old companions, still in their primitive costume and slaving for others, while he was independent, and then holding the rolled tobacco between two fingers and turning on his heel he would say, " Only a lot of savages, anyway," and then go back to his comfortable home. The point in the joke was that of the crowd the Fox himself was the least likely to change in a hurry. He was said to be able to transform himself in case of necessity into a fox ; that is, the " spirit of his dream "—the power to whom he was under vow—had given him assurance that in his hour of extremity this spirit would come to his help, and enable him to thus change his visible appearance—the man Fox would become the animal fox in shape. This, it was told me, had actually taken place, and an eye-witness thus describes the circumstance:

" The Fox and four others of us started out in the late autumn to steal horses or take scalps from the Blackfeet. The Fox was our leader and conjurer. He was ever and anon to look into the unknown and determine our course and movements. We left our camps between the Battle River and the North Saskatchewan, and travelled south for several days. We crossed the Red Deer below the big canyon, and keeping on came to the track of a large camp of Blackfeet travelling southerly. Now we began to move with extreme caution, and when south of Service Berry Creek I went on alone to scout, as the tracks were fresh, my companions remaining hidden while I was away. After a long, stealthy run I came in sight of the camp of the enemy, and taking stock of it and its locality, I went back to my companions, thinking to inspire them with great enthusiasm because of what I had seen; but though I sang the war song as I approached them, they did not stir, and I saw a gloom was upon the party.

"Then the Fox spoke up and said, 'I am sorry, but it is no use; we must return from here. The Spirit has informed me that it would be utter ruin for us to advance. We must retrace our steps.' I was loath to do this. I wanted horses, and I upbraided Fox with deceiving us; but he was determined, as he said, to follow the guidance of the one he dreamt of, and finally I reluctantly joined my comrades, who had already started on the back trail. Sullenly and in quiet we moved northward. Presently the Fox began to limp, and finally sat down, saying, 'There is something in my knee; see if you can find a thorn or a splinter.' We could not find any such thing, and yet his knee was swollen and inflamed, and soon he could not put his foot to the ground. He said to us repeatedly, 'Leave me, let me die alone.' But we would not listen to that. I made him a crutch, and we moved on slowly, very slowly. We helped him from time to time, but his leg grew worse, and was terribly swollen. And now winter came upon us, and snow and cold increased. When we reached the Red Deer it was frozen out on both sides, and the channel was full of float ice. I said, 'I will cross first and have a fire ready for you.' So I stripped, forded the river, and made a camp on the north side in a clump of spruce. When this was ready, I shouted to my companions to come across. They took a long pole, and put the Fox in the centre, and all holding on to the pole waded abreast through the current and float ice, and thus brought our lame conjurer over. The snow was now deep and we were out of provisions. The next morning my brother and myself went to hunt for game, and we had not gone far when we saw tracks in the snow, which turned out to be those of buffalo. I succeeded in killing two, and our party packed all of the meat into our camp, and we busied ourselves in cutting up and drying this meat for our journey.

"In the meantime the Fox's leg was growing

worse, and he implored us to abandon him, but we could not do this. Then I fixed a strap of buffalo-hide to go across his shoulder, and fastening this to two crutches, we made another start. Climbing the steep banks of the Red Deer, and with many stops, we continued our way homeward. Our course was along the Buffalo Lake. One day we heard shooting in the distance, and scouting for the cause, found that the Sarcee camp was right in our way. This was very disappointing, as it compelled us to make a big detour to avoid this camp and its many hunters. Very slowly and stealthily we travelled among our enemies. There was no chance to steal horses, as the snow was too deep and our party too weak. They could track us at once, and then, situated as we were, our scalps would certainly be theirs. Several times we were nearly discovered, but the weather being cold and stormy, and at times misty, favored us, and we had got about opposite the camp one day when my brother filled a pipe, and handing it to the Fox, said to him: 'Here, smoke that and call upon your source of help, for you need this now, as we are likely to be tracked or seen at any time.' So the Fox smoked the pipe, and said, 'Well, leave me here alone and hurry on to yonder woods. Do not look back, but wait for me when you reach the woods.'

"We left him and ran across the plain. I was ahead and did not look back, but as we ran all of a sudden I heard my brother cry out, 'Alas! alas! I have injured the Fox,' and without looking back, I said, 'What is it?' And my brother told me that he had looked back and seen the Fox coming on the dead run after us, but while he looked he saw him fall, as if struck down, and then he knew he had broken the charm or influence by his disobedience.

"When we reached the woods we waited, and after a long time the Fox crawled up and at once charged us with looking back. 'I was coming on nicely when you looked back and spoiled me by your foolish curiosity.' My brother confessed at once that it was he who had done this, but said he was prompted to do so, as he thought we had left our friend alone, and our enemies might come upon him at any time. After this the Fox got worse, and his foot and all of his leg was fearfully swollen; and yet I could not find any sight of a bealing or gathering of matter. After days of slow progress the weather became milder, and in some spots on the hills the snow went off. One day we came out upon the valley which is called, 'Where the buffalo hunters meet in running,' and we sat down on the hill above the valley. Here, I thought, I will try the Fox, and see if there is anything in his boasted association with the spirits. So I filled a pipe, and lighting it, said to him, 'Here, smoke this, and listen to me. You brought us out on this trip, you promised us horses, you led us to depend on your spiritual power; you have deceived us in every way, and for many days you have been a burden to us. Many times our lives have been in danger because of you. Why continue this any longer? Why not invoke the help you profess to be able to call to your aid? Do this now.' Then the Fox said, 'Your words are true, and you should have left me to die long ago, but you would not. I have been a burden and a danger to you. I will do as you say; possibly I may be heard.'

"Baring his back, he said, 'Here, paint a fox on my back with this yellow earth. Let my head represent his head, let his forelegs go down on to my arms, and his hind legs on to my thighs. Make my head and back yellow, then take some powder and wet it, and darken the lower parts of his limbs and tail, and my nose and mouth, and take a little white earth and tip the tail.' I and my companions did as he told us. Then he said, 'Cross the valley, climb the hill; just over its brow wait for me, but mind, as you cross the valley and climb the hill, do not look back—remember that.' Then he held the pipe on high, and began to chant his invocation song, and thus we left him; nor did we look back as we ran across the valley, in which the buffalo were standing on both sides of us like a black wall. Climbing the hill, we went over its brow, and made a circle so as to command our track, and there waited. We were intensely anxious. By-and-bye we saw a stir among the buffalo in the valley, and then we discerned a small object coming on our track. It looked in the distance like a kit fox, then, when nearer, it appeared like an ordinary red fox. On it came at the gallop, and, keeping our track, climbed the hill, and was soon on its brow, and presently opposite to us. We were now in full view; then it saw us, and the Fox himself rose up, saying, 'Ah, you caught me in my other self.'

"We did not say anything, we were so astonished. The Fox walked over to us as if there were nothing the matter with him. His leg, which had been big and swollen, was now down to its usual size. He pulled down his legging and said to me, 'Here, lance this, and I will be all right.' Sure enough, there was a bag of matter on his knee, but the swelling was gone. So I took an arrow, sharpened the point, bound it around with string a little distance from the point, and with this lanced his knee, from which the matter poured forth. Then I made a ring of twisted grass, bound this over the wound, and we continued our journey. The Fox delayed us no more, and in a few days was entirely recovered."

Though well-nigh forty years have passed since the above experience, three out of the five actors are still living, and they say they must believe what they saw and felt.

Another of our friends was called "The-Camp-is-Moving." He would shake his powder-horn and it would never empty. Like the widow's cruse of oil, it would replenish. It was said he had but to sing and shake his horn, and powder came at his bidding.

Once "Mr. The-Camp-is-Moving" came to me at Pigeon Lake and begged for some shot. "You know," said he, "I am all right as to powder," giving his powder-horn a significant shake; and I ventured to say that it might be easier to make shot than powder, that if I could make powder I would try making shot also. "Ah, my grandchild," said the old man, "we must not be presuming. I am thankful it is given to me to make powder." After that what could I do but give him some shot. This same old man had a fashion of dying, or going into a trance, and to bring him out of this his brother conjurers had to gather to his tent, and bringing their drums and rattles, sing his own songs, which after a time would result in the old man's coming back to earth, when he would have wonderful things to tell his people. These men I have mentioned, and others widely differing from us in creed, were yet friendly and kind in their attitude to the members of our mission party.

CHAPTER XX.

Victoria becomes a Hudson's Bay trading post—An adventure on a raft—The annual fresh meat hunt organized—Among the buffalo—Oliver misses his shot and is puzzled—My experience with a runaway horse—A successful hunt—My "bump of locality" surprises Peter—Home again.

THE Indians, both Wood and Plain, pagan and Christian, were now flocking into Victoria in such numbers that the Hudson's Bay Company saw the necessity of establishing a trading post there. I was offered the charge of this, but father did not seem to relish the idea, so it dropped, and a Mr. Flett was sent to put up buildings and open trade with the Indians. Mr. Flett was a native of the Red River settlement, and thoroughly understood the Indians and their language. He was a warm friend of our mission, later on himself becoming an honored missionary of the Presbyterian Church to the Indians in another part of the country.

Victoria had now (in 1864) the beginning of a Christian mission and the starting of a

Hudson's Bay post, and was becoming known as a place on the Saskatchewan. For the month or six weeks that the large camps were there, spring and fall, it was a busy point. Travellers, traders, hunters and freighters were coming and going every little while all through the year. Already this new place had become the nucleus of a Christian civilization. One Hudson's Bay packet once in the year, and an occasional budget of mail by some unexpected traveller, were our sole means of communication with the outside world. In this matter we were farther away than Hong Kong or Bombay.

As autumn merged into winter, the larger number of the Indians recrossed the Saskatchewan and struck for the buffalo. In the meantime some of us were busy getting out more timber and lumber. One night, when most of the Indians had gone, Peter, Oliver and I were coming down the river on a raft of timber. We had left early the previous morning, expecting to be back by evening, and therefore had not taken bedding with us. The carrying, rolling and handspiking of the timber to the water's edge, and the making of our raft, had kept us late, so before starting we put some earth on the raft, and throwing dry wood on this, as soon as the night grew cold we made a fire. When about half way home, while passing through a

"Tying our clothes in bundles above our heads, we started into the ice-cold current." (*Page 215.*)

ripple, our raft grounded on the rocks, and do what we would in the night we could not get it off. Having neither provisions nor bedding, and our supply of wood on the raft but small, we concluded to wade or swim ashore. The river was broad, the distance to the shore long, and the depth uncertain.

Undressing, and tying our clothes in bundles above our heads, we started into the ice-cold current. Slowly we felt our way, for the bottom was full of boulders and stones, and irregular in depth. As I was the shortest of our party I came near having to swim. Down I went, and deeper still, until all but my head was submerged. Stepping slowly and carefully on my toes I made my way, longing for the shore. Many a river have I swam and waded in all kinds of weather, but that long, slow trip from raft to shore in the dark night, made darker still by the sombre shadows of the high wooded banks, I shall never forget. After an interminable time, as it seemed, we reached the shore and stepped out with bare feet and naked bodies on to the rough, stony beach, and into the keen, frosty air. But what a glow we were in when we did have our clothes on once more! We were in prime condition for a sharp run, and it did not take us long, inured as we were, to climb the steep bank and run the three or four miles to the mission house. The next day we towed a skiff to where our raft was, worked it off the rocks, and brought it down home.

As the cold weather set in, it became necessary to organize for the "fresh meat hunt." In an isolated interior place like Victoria, where there are neither waggon nor cart makers, nor yet harness makers; where your wheels are wooden and your axles ironless, and wood grinds on wood; where your harness is of the skins of the wild animals around you, crudely and roughly home-made, it means something to get ready for a trip where you expect to find heavy loads and frozen ground, with winter perhaps setting in before you again reach home. To mend carts and harness, to hunt up horses and oxen, to transport your vehicles and equipment over a wide river in a small skiff, to swim your stock through the cold water—all of this takes some time and causes a great deal of hard work. But we must have the meat, and so in good time we are rolling south, hunters, running horses and cart drivers, all eager for the first glimpse of the buffalo.

This time our course was more westerly, and on the third day we had our first run, near the "cross woods," on the plain which stretches from within a few miles of Victoria to the Battle River. Our chief hunters were " Muddy

Bull" and Peter. The rest of us were kept busy butchering and hauling into camp, moving camp, guarding stock, providing wood, etc. From before daylight until late at night we were all on the jump, Sunday being our only rest, and then we took turns in guarding our stock. To work hard all day, and then guard stock and camp all night, those long fall nights, made one very "gapish" the next day, and gave him sound sleep the following night. In all this father took his share, and upon him rested the chief responsibility of the expedition. On these trips as much haste as was consistent with the success of the object in view was made in order to be as short a period as possible away from the mission, which was during this time almost without any human protection.

My man Oliver, though a native of the Red River Settlement, and thus born in the great North-West, had never until now seen buffalo. In fact, all the experiences of this last summer had been new to him. We left him in charge of camp one morning, and went out some miles after buffalo. When towards evening I came in on a cart-load of meat, he exclaimed: "What kept you so long? I have been waiting to go for my buffalo."

"Where are your buffalo?" I asked.

"Oh! just over yon hill," he answered.

"How many have you?" was my next question.

"I don't know," was the answer.

"How is that?" I queried.

"Well," said Oliver, "a big band of buffalo came down to the creek near camp, and I jumped on the bay colt and charged them up yonder slope. There were hundreds of them, and just as they went over the ridge I fired into them, and I am sure there must be five or six dead buffalo lying over there."

"Did you see any dead ones?" I asked.

"No," said he, "for I hurried back to look after things, and have been anxiously waiting for some one to relieve me, so I might go and bring in my buffalo."

As it was only a little way, I told Oliver to jump on one of the horses and see if there were any dead buffalo over the ridge. Presently he came back, quietly wondering how he could have missed the big herd. Many a man has had a similar experience. Over a rough country, with horse at full jump, inexperienced men have fired many a shot, and never even hit the carcase of a big bull. Then, as to killing more than one at a shot, this was seldom done. I have heard of an Indian in the Beaver Hills killing two bulls at one shot, and when his comrade came over the hill, and saw the two dead animals, he asked, "How is this? you fired but one shot." "Yes," said the other, "I did wait for some time to get three in a line, but finally had to be satisfied with two." This same fellow was possessed of some dry wit, for his friend asked him, as he was leaving the fire for a little, to turn his roast, if it needed turning; and when he came back the bare spit was over the fire, and the meat at the other end on the ground. "What is this?" he asked, with a touch of indignation in his voice. "What is the matter?" responded the wag. "You requested me to turn your roast, and I did so," and the victim had to swallow the joke. But it was harder to make Oliver understand how he could miss hundreds of buffalo bunched up as these were, and he could not but refer to this strange event ever and anon all the evening. Many a banter did he get from the rest of our party about his dead buffalo. "Where are you going?" one would shout to another, and the answer would come back, "After Oliver's buffalo."

I had quite an experience the same afternoon in coming back to camp with my load of meat. The rather wild horse I was driving somehow or other shook off his bridle and started across the prairie at a gallop on his own course. So long as the plain was only slightly undulating this did not very much disturb me, but presently we came to buffalo trails and badger holes, and thump, bump, thump went the wooden cart, and piece by piece out tumbled the meat, and I began to speculate how long the cart would hold together. Then I saw we were making straight for the banks of a creek, where a decided smash would be inevitable.

I could have jumped out behind, and let the whole thing go, but I was loath to do this, so I finally mustered up courage to climb out on the brute's back. This only made him the more frantic for a while, but presently I got a line over his nose, and, slapping his head, turned his course to smooth ground, and finally stopped the excited animal. I then got things fixed up, drove back along the course of our wild race, gathered up my meat, and thus brought horse and cart, meat and self, without much damage, to camp.

In those days we seldom bothered with the hides. Now and then we took some specially good ones and used them on the way home to cover the meat, and later on had them dressed; but generally, with the exception of what we used to mend carts or harness, we left the hides on the plain. Our need was meat, and for this we required the utmost capacity of our transport.

"Slapping his head, I turned his course to smooth ground."
(*Page 224.*)

On the third evening, after we got fairly among the buffalo, our carts were loaded, and we felt that we had been successful indeed. No lives lost, no limbs broken, no horses stolen. Our hunters had ridden without hurt over thousands of badger holes, across many miles of rough country, and amongst hundreds of wild, strong buffalo. Our cart drivers had gone in every direction, across country, to and fro, butchering the slain, and hauling in the meat to camp. Hundreds of great grey wolves, and—to judge by the yelping—thousands of coyotes, had howled and snarled and fought all about us both day and night. Yet in a very short time we were loaded, all safe and sound; and feelingly we sang our praise, and father voiced our thanksgiving ere we retired to rest that night.

It was on this hunt that Peter woke up to the fact that I had been born with the natural gift of a large " bump of locality." Three of us —" Muddy Bull," Peter and myself—charged a bunch of buffalo. Peter had a long flint-lock gun and a big percussion six-shooting revolver. I happened to be riding alongside of him when he fired his gun, and now that he pulled the revolver, the gun was in the way; so he handed it to me. Presently in the rush we were separated, and here I was with two guns. Not caring to be so hampered, as gently as I could I flung Peter's gun to the ground; but in doing so noticed the locality. Fortunately, also, I saw "Muddy Bull" directly opposite, about two hundred yards distant, knock a cow down. She could not get up, for I could see that he had broken her back. This was another mark to me, and I charged my memory with it as on we rushed in the mad race. By-and-bye I came across Peter some two miles from there, and the first question was, "Where is my gun?" "I threw it away, back yonder," I answered, and Peter blessed me warmly, declaring we would never find that gun again; and it did look like it, for here was all out doors and a thousand places looking alike. However, I took him straight back to his gun. He could hardly believe his own eyes, but as he picked it up he said, "You will do for the North-West."

The next day our carts were creaking and squealing with their heavy loads on the home stretch. In the meantime winter was steadily creeping on. The ground was frozen, the ice on the lakes becoming thick and strong, and the nights were cold. If you were on guard, you felt the necessity of quick action to keep warm. If you were asleep under the carts, you very reluctantly turned out at four o'clock a.m. to gather up bedding, etc., hitch up your share of the brigade, and trudge on through the cold until near daylight, when you stopped for breakfast; but, as this was the regular thing, you soon came to the conclusion that the chicken-hearted and weak-willed had no place in this keenly new land—so new that the polish of nature was still bright and thick all over it.

In a little more than two weeks from our start on the hunt, we are again letting our loads down the steep southern bank of the Saskatchewan, and yonder the smoke from the mission house chimneys and the ear-flaps of a few buffalo skin lodges meets our eyes, curling heavenward. I say "curling heavenward" because I have been bred to do so, but who knows where heaven is, especially when one thinks that what was up a little while ago, is down now? This time we ford our stock through a ripple, about half a mile below the mission, which is infinitely better than swimming them through the floating ice-cakes which are being hurried eastward by the rapid current. Then comes the hard and cold work of crossing carts and loads in the skiff; but finally the whole thing is done, and the product of our fall hunt is on the stage, and will become a prominent factor in the working of the mission for the next two months, unless an extra lot of starving people come upon us.

CHAPTER XXI.

Father and I visit Fort Edmonton—Peter takes to himself a wife—Mr. Connor becomes school teacher—First school in that part of the country—Culinary operations—Father decides to open a mission at Pigeon Lake—I go prospecting—Engage a Roman Catholic guide—Our guide's sudden "illness"—Through new scenes—Reach Pigeon Lake—Getting out timber for building—Incidents of return trip.

SHORTLY after this I accompanied father and Peter to Edmonton. We left Friday morning and reached Edmonton the evening of the next day; spent Sunday, Monday, and part of Tuesday there, and were back at Victoria Wednesday night. The distance to and from Edmonton by the bridle-trail (for there was, as yet, no cart or waggon road on the north side of the river) was one hundred and eighty miles. Edmonton was then without a single settler, and unless you met or overtook some traveller or wandering Indian, you and your party, large or small, were entirely alone. Father was practically chaplain of the Fort, as his predecessors had been, but these visits meant more than this, for

Edmonton was a centre, and ever and anon messengers from the camps came in there, and thus the missionary could send messages and counsel and keep in touch with a people scattered over a large area.

Back once more at home we found plenty to do in making ready for winter. There were cattle to provide for and look after, horses to keep track of, dogs to feed, wood to cut, haul, and again split up at the door, timber to take out, and lumber to saw, dry, plane, groove and tongue. In the meantime Peter married a Whitefish Lake woman and brought her to the mission. She was a fine-looking Christian woman, and we all felt like congratulating our friend on his good fortune.

Mr. Connor, who came up with me from the Red River in the summer, and whom I left some time since building a shack for the winter, took the work of harvesting and threshing our small field of barley on shares, and now has engaged to teach school for the winter months. Our shanty is to be the school-room, and Mr. Steinhauer's children, from Whitefish Lake, our family, and a few orphan Indian children, are to be the scholars. This will be the first institution of the kind in this part of the North-West. Our house is full and our larder precarious, but father and mother do not hesitate for a moment, but freely open their house to the children of a brother missionary, who otherwise would be without any such means of education. Moreover, father has accepted the little daughter of " Chief Child," who in dying besought him to take his much loved child, and train her in a Christian home. Thus our home will send nine scholars to the new school, and for the winter mother's responsibility will have increased greatly, while we who have to provide food for such an household will of necessity need to keep on the move.

Our garden this year had given us a nice quantity of potatoes, and we have some barley, but meat will be our chief food. As we have no mill, the only way we can prepare barley is to soak it, and then, when partially dry, pound it in a wooden mortar to loosen the chaff and husks, and then winnow this. We boil the barley in soup, or else parch it and then grind it in our small coffee-mill, and make cake of the meal obtained, all of which is slow and tedious work. So long as we can get buffalo within three hundred miles we would prefer buffalo-steaks to barley-meal.

The winter of 1864-5 came in bright and fine; clear, cold weather, but no snow or storm. In my spare time I broke in a train of young dogs. When I left Norway House, in 1862, I left at home a fine train of dogs. One of these, a handsome animal, my sisters had named "Maple." She had just enough of the "husky" strain of blood to make her hardy and strong. When father moved up in 1863 he brought Maple along, and that same autumn she made a den in the bank in front of the shanty and brought forth a fine litter of pups. Mother and the girls had taken good care of these, and they grew into strong, handsome dogs. They were now one year old, and I took pleasure in breaking them for the sled. Many a long run we had on the bare, frozen ground. My plan was to hitch the pups to a toboggan, and attached to this I had a long line, the end of which I kept in my hand, and as I ran behind I could, when I said "Whoa," stop the dogs. Soon they learned all the words of command, which, by the way, are but four. Then by holding the line I could regulate their step, and soon I had them trained down to trot a mile in a very short time. As I urged them forward, if any should break trot I would hold back on the line and pull the whole train into a regular step. My, how those pups did trot! Their legs would go like drumsticks, and I was proud of my success. By using them carefully this their first winter, if they lived they would make flyers. This was the opinion of experts. Father, mother, the girls, everybody in the settlement, all took a great interest in those pups. At last I got them down so that they could trot as fast as I could run, and that was making good time.

About the first of December snow came, and father put into execution a project he had been thinking about for some time, and that was to begin a mission west of Edmonton, between that post and the mountains. He had about decided on Pigeon Lake as a suitable spot, so he told me he wanted me to look up the place, and, if feasible, take out some timber for a house, as he proposed to do something in the coming spring in the way of permanent occupancy. The Mountain and Wood Stoneys, and some Wood Crees, who frequented that country, were without a missionary. Accordingly, early in December, I took Oliver with me and started with two trains of dogs, carrying loads of dried provisions. In two days we reached Edmonton, where I hoped to secure a guide who could take me straight to Pigeon Lake; but there were very few Indians or half-breeds around the Fort, and only one who had ever been at Pigeon Lake. I hired this fellow at once, and we were to start as soon as the Fort gates were open the next morning.

During the evening I went around to see how my guide was progressing in making ready for a start in the morning, when lo! I found him both sick and lame. This man, a few hours since all right and glad of the work offered, was now sick, lame and totally unable to travel. I thought this strange, and set to work to find out the secret cause of such a change. I pretty soon found that his spiritual adviser was at the bottom of it. He had put his foot on our enterprise, nipping it in the bud, as he thought. So I went back to my man and told him it was all up with our guide. "Will we go back?" enquired Oliver. "No, sir," I said; "we will find Pigeon Lake, notwithstanding all the priests in Canada. Let us go to bed," which we did, and with the creaking of the heavy gates on their hinges in the morning we drove out of the Fort on our quest. The plan I had formed in the night was to follow a trail which led from Edmonton to the Mountain House, until we came to Battle River, then follow this up to Pigeon Creek, which ran out of Pigeon Lake. We would follow the creek up to the lake, and coast along the shore until I found the spot where it was proposed to establish a mission.

This was a long distance around, but (D.V.) I had no doubt of succeeding. Away we went, all day on the west-bound trail, and camped for the night in a clump of spruce. Then, as the track could be plainly seen, we were off before daylight, and ere noon came upon a new-made road crossing ours at right angles. Here I stopped and pondered. Perhaps this road comes from Pigeon Lake. If it does it will save us four or five days' journey in going and coming. Finally I said to Oliver, "Here goes, we will take this trail and follow it until to-morrow night, or to its end; and at the worst we can come back and take up our original plan." So we turned up the new road and carried on faster than ever. All the way from Edmonton had been through a country entirely new to me. Now we were going into the forest, and travelling almost due west. When it came time to camp for the night, after selecting a suitable place and pulling my dogs out of their collars, I left Oliver to make camp, and running some distance climbed a tree and took a survey of the country. It was all forest and no sign of a lake to be seen. Next morning we were away early, and by noon had climbed a range of hills covered with dense timber. On reaching the summit we noticed a big depression not far ahead, and thought this might be the lake, which it proved to be, for in about an hour we were on the ice, and driving across the bay were at our destination.

The Indians had made a cache and left some fish, and we considered ourselves fortunate in having these for our dogs. We spent the rest of the day in fixing up a camp. Next morning we went to work taking out timber, and in three days had nearly enough for two modest houses. We had not far to haul it, our dogs were quick, and we were both of us fairly good axemen. We had found the lake, had taken out the timber, and hauled it to the spot, and now, cacheing our provisions, we took some fish instead, and started about two o'clock one moonlight morning on our return trip. The rest and the change of diet had done our dogs good, and my old Draffan rang his bells in grand style as we followed the narrow trail through the forest, which crackled about us, for Jack Frost was now vigorously at work.

In the meantime snow had fallen, and the roads were heavier; nevertheless we made Edmonton the same evening before the gates closed, and every Protestant in the Fort was glad we had found Pigeon Lake. Eighty miles at least in the time we had taken was considered good travelling. We spent most of the next day with friends at the Fort, and in the evening, just before the gates closed, drove out some five miles and camped for the night. Starting early next morning we made a trail through several inches of new snow, and pushing on made Victoria that evening, which was a better day than the one from Pigeon Lake to Edmonton. We took to the river at the mouth of the Sturgeon, and followed it all the way to the mission. When opposite the mouth of Sucker Creek, just a little while before dark, we boiled our kettle and ate some pemmican; then as I had run ahead all day, Oliver took his turn at the lead, but within a mile old Draffan passed him, and kept the lead himself the rest of the way. From point to point, prudently avoiding the open holes and dangerous spots, the wise old dog carried on for home, and between seven and eight we had reached the mission house. Father expressed himself as delighted with our report of the trip. We had found the lake, got out the timber, cached the provisions, and in a sense started the new mission.

In the meantime those at home were preparing for the erection of a church in the spring, and Peter was making lumber as fast as this could be done by whip-sawing; we hauling the logs to the saw-pit at odd times between trips.

CHAPTER XXII.

Another buffalo hunt—Visit Maskepetoon's camp—The old chief's plucky deed—Arrival of a peace party from the Blackfeet—A "peace dance"—Buffalo in plenty—Our mysterious visitor—A party of Blackfeet come upon us—Watching and praying—Arrive home with well-loaded sleds—Christmas festivities.

THERE had been no attempt to make a fishery that fall, and as our stock of meat was now growing small, father thought I had better go out to the plains and see how things were among the Indians, and if possible bring in a supply of meat. Accordingly, very soon after coming from Pigeon Lake, I arranged a party for this purpose. Old Joseph, whom the reader will have become familiar with, and a young Indian named "Tommy" went with me. We had four trains of dogs, the Indians one each while I had two, for I was taking "Maple" and her pups for their first "business" trip. James Connor also came with us on his own account.

The third day out we came to Maskepetoon's camp, and found the Indians full of another of the old Chief's plucky deeds. During the late fall and early winter, the Blackfeet had become exceedingly troublesome. They were continually harassing the Wood Cree camp, until at last Maskepetoon determined to go with a party to the Blackfeet camp to arrange, if possible, a temporary peace which might last over the winter months, and thus give the Crees an opportunity to make robes and provisions for trade and home use. As winter advanced the buffalo had come north rapidly, and the Blackfeet tribes had of necessity to follow them. Fearful destitution had been the result to some of the large camps. They had eaten their dogs and begun upon their horses before they reached the south fringe of the large herds that were moving north into the rich and well-sheltered areas of the Saskatchewan country.

It was well known in Maskepetoon's camp that the Blackfeet were in strength not more than one hundred miles south, and that the Bloods and Piegans were within easy distance beyond them; but Maskepetoon had great faith in his record with these people, and at the head of a small party he set out to patch up a peace, even if it should be but short-lived. While on this expedition his little party was charged upon by a strong body of Blackfeet who were coming north on the war-path. Such was their

"Maskepetoon calmly . . . took out his Cree Testament . . . and began to read." (*Page 239.*)

number and the vigor and dash of their charge that, as they drew near, Maskepetoon's little company fled, all but himself and his grandson, a boy some fifteen or sixteen years of age. These alone stood the wild onslaught of their enemies. The veteran chief and the noble boy of like heroic blood stood like statues "when all but they had fled." Maskepetoon calmly put his hand in his bosom and took out his Cree Testament, and then coolly fixing on his glasses, opened and began to read. The grandson, in relating to us the incident afterwards, said, "There was no tremor in his voice; it was as if grandfather was reading to us in the quiet of his own tent."

In the meantime the Blackfeet came on apace, and hoping to take their victims alive, refrained from firing a gun or speeding an arrow. Then they saw the majestic old man, indifferent to them, engaged in looking into something he held in his hand: "What manner of man is this?" "What is he doing?" "What is that he is holding in his hands?" They had seen flint-lock guns, and flint and steel-shod arrows, and battle-axes and scalping knives in men's hands under similar circumstances, but they had never beheld a New Testament. Thunderstruck they paused in the midst of their wild rush, and stared in utter astonishment. Presently the elders amongst them said to one another in whispers, "It is Mon-e-guh-ba-now" (the Young Chief), and then they began to shout, "Mon-e-guh-ba-now!" and this grand old man (for, blessed be the Lord, no nation or place has a monopoly of the qualities of true manhood) quietly looked up and in response to their shout, replied, "Yes, I am Mon-e-guh-ba-now." Then they rushed upon him with joy, and their leader, embracing him, said: "Our hearts are glad to make peace with you, Mon-e-guh-ba-now. You are a brave man. I am proud and glad to be the leader of a party that meets you thus. What is that you hold in your hand?" Maskepetoon told him that it was the word of the "Great Spirit," and the Blackfoot warrior said, "That explains your conduct. It is His will that we should meet as brothers to-day." And there on the snow-covered plain, these men, who by heredity and life-long habit were deadly enemies, smoked and talked and planned for peace. It was arranged that each party should return to their own people, and that if the Blackfeet desired peace they should send an embassy to the Cree camp; Maskepetoon giving his word as a guarantee for the safety of those who might be sent on this embassage.

This had occurred a few days before our arrival in camp, and the Blackfeet were looked for at any time. Sure enough, we were hardly settled in Muddy Bull's hospitable lodge, when a scout reached camp, and announced that a party of Blackfeet were in sight. This threw the camp into a state of great excitement, and speculation was rife as to whether Maskepetoon would be able to make good his promise of safety. There were hundreds in that camp who lusted and thirsted for the blood of these men; many a boy or girl who had lost a father or mother or both; many a woman who had lost lover or husband; many parents who had lost their children at the hands of the people represented by these men who were now approaching camp. Many of these felt down in their hearts that this would be a fine opportunity to slake some of their thirst for revenge. Maskepetoon knew this full well. He at once sent his son out to meet the embassy, and attend them into camp, and in the meantime arranged his trusted men all through the camp to be ready to forestall any outbreak of frenzied hate.

I ran out to see the incoming of the Blackfeet. Young Maskepetoon had arranged an escort. These men were on horseback, and ranged on either side of the Blackfeet, who were on foot. The latter were seven in number, big, fine-looking fellows, but one could see that they were under a heavy strain, and that it needed all their will power to nerve them up to the occasion. With regular and solemn step, in single file, they came, and as they walked they sang what I supposed was intended for a peace song. Young Maskepetoon took them straight to his father's lodge, and at once it was arranged to hold a reception meeting and a "peace dance."

It was now evening, and at supper I enquired of old Joseph what he thought of my attending this dance. He said he was not going himself, but he thought Maskepetoon would like to have me there, and that I had better go and see for myself, so as to learn all I could about the Indians, for only in this way would I get to understand them. Accordingly, when the drums beat to announce the dance, I went, and was given a seat between Maskepetoon and the Blackfeet. Two large lodges had been put together to make room, but the main body of the company looked on from the outside.

After a few short speeches the dancing began. Four men drummed and sang, and an Indian sprang into the ring, between the fire and the guests, leaped, jumped and whooped with great spirit, and presently gave his blanket to one of the Blackfeet. Then another did likewise, except that he varied the gift. This time it was his beaded shot-pouch and powder-horn, and strings also. Each one, it would seem, had his own peculiar dance. Then another would leap into the ring with several articles, and as he danced to the strong singing and vigorous drumming of the orchestra, he would give to a Blackfoot his contributions to this peace meeting. Then the drummers ceased for a little and the conductor shouted out: "The Sloping Bank is strong for peace. He had but one blanket, and he has given that." "The Red Sky Bird means what he says. He had but one gun, and he has given that." And again the leader tapped his drum, and the orchestra burst forth, and another and another dancer took the floor. Then a couple of young fellows, in fantastic costume, gave us the "buffalo dance," and did some tall jumping, such as would have pleased one of those "highly cultured audiences" in one of our eastern cities.

Presently my friend Mr. Starving Young Bull (the gentleman who had honored me with an invitation to the dedication feast in his new lodge), took the floor. He was no small man, this Mr. Starving Young Bull. He had several new blankets on his shoulders, and a brand-new flint-lock gun in his hand, and as he danced and whooped and kept time to the furious drumming, he gave his gun to one of the Blackfeet as he whirled past him, and again gave one of the new blankets to another, and so on until he had spent all his gifts and strength, and sat down naked and tired, while the chief singer shouted out his name, and said, "The Starving Young Bull is a great man. He dances well and long. He goes in for peace strongly. He has given all his blankets and is naked; he has given his one gun, and is without arms himself," and the crowd sent up a chorus of applause which my friend drank in and was pleased, as many another man has been when the crowd cheered.

The Blackfeet also in turn danced, and gave presents of what they had, and thus the peace dance went on. Long before it ended, however, I had slipped away to our camp and retired to rest, as we had travelled some distance that day and expected to travel farther on the morrow. We had heard of buffalo coming in from the south-east, and the Indians were waiting for them to pass on to the north, when they hoped to build pounds, and thus slaughter them wholesale. We promised to go around the head of the approaching herds, and not interfere with the projected plan. This would give us a longer trip, but it was the right thing to do.

The next day we travelled through a wild storm, and camped in the rolling hills, which in that part of the country are seemingly without number. The next day the storm still raged, but on we travelled, and about noon came upon the buffalo. Killing a couple, we camped, and waited for a lull in the weather, which came that night. Next morning (Saturday) the sky was clear and the weather cold and crisp, but Tommy and I succeeded in killing enough buffalo to load and furnish provisions for men and dogs. That afternoon I made a chance shot, and killed a fine cow at a very long range with my smooth-bore gun. She fell dead in her tracks, and when we butchered the animal, we failed to find where the ball had struck; but later, when Joseph was arranging the head to roast by our camp fire, he found that my ball had entered the ear.

We moved camp into a bluff of timber about the centre of our "kill," and while Joseph and Jim made camp and chopped and carried wood, Tommy and I hauled in the meat, which work kept us busy until near midnight. Then we had to stage it up and freeze it into shape for our narrow dog-sleds, as also in the interim keep it away from the dogs. Fortunately there was fine moonlight to aid us in our labor. Joseph worked like a good fellow at packing in logs to our woodpile, until the stars told him it was midnight and Sunday morning had begun. The night was one of keen cold, and the crisp snow creaked as the buffalo, either in herds or singly, passed to the windward of our camp. Scores of wolves and coyotes barked and howled around us. Every little while our dogs would make a short rush at some of these that ventured too near, and yet we were so tired that not buffalo nor wolves nor the possibility of strange Indians being near, nor yet the severe cold of our open camp, upon which gusts of wintry wind ever and anon played, could deter us from sleeping on into the clear frosty Sabbath morning which all too soon came upon us.

We made up our fire, cooked our food, sang some hymns, joined in prayer, with old Joseph leading, then thawed some meat and cut it up into morsels to feed our dogs. Alternately toasting or freezing as we sat or stood before that big camp-fire, which in turn we replenished and stirred and poked, we passed the morning hours. About noon the wind again blew up into a storm, and soon clouds of snow were swirling in every direction. We, in the comparative shelter of our carefully picked camp, were congratulating ourselves on the storm, for would it not cover our tracks, which diverged and converged to and from our temporary home for miles on every side, and had been as a big "give away" to any roaming band of hostile men. We were rather glad to hear the soughing and gusting of the wild winds, for there seemed to come with these a strange sense of security

"This strange Indian, without looking at us, sang on." (*Page 247.*)

which was comforting. But alas for merely human calculation, even then the wily Blackfeet were closing in on us. We were just sitting down to our dinner when, with a weird, strange chanting song there came in out of the storm into the shelter of the camp a tall, wild-looking Blackfoot. We knew he was not alone. We knew that even then each one of us was covered by the gun or shod-arrow of his companions. Right across from us, beside our camp-fire, this strange Indian, without looking at us, sang on. I looked at my companions. Tommy was pale; Jim was white. Like myself, each was grasping his gun with one hand. I could not see myself, but I could feel my heart-beats, and it seemed as if my hair was lifting under my cap. It was a great stimulator to turn to Joseph, who was coolly eating his dinner. Not a muscle changed. Not the faintest appearance of a change of blood showed in his face. Like the stolid philosopher he was, he continued his meal.

The Blackfoot, having finished his song, made a short speech. Not a word all this time was uttered on our side. In silence (save for the sound of Joseph crunching his meat) we sat—verily, for three in the party it was a solemn time. Then our visitor, having finished his harangue, disappeared as he came, and I said to Joseph, who understood the language, "What did he say?" Old Joseph swallowed a mouthful of meat, cleared his throat, and said: "He says there are many of them; their hearts are for peace, and they will come into our camp."

Presently they did come, some forty in all. Ten to one they stood around us, and I told them, through Joseph, about their friends we had met in Maskepetoon's camp, and how they had been treated; that the people in the north were all for peace; that it was our work to teach all men that peace and brotherhood was the right thing; that if they wished to camp beside us, we would share our meat with them; that the reason we were not travelling was this was the "God day," and we did not travel or hunt on that day; that the Indians who were with me were the near friends of Mon-e-guh-ba-now, and that Mon-e-guh-ba-now was my personal friend. Then the leader spoke up and said: "We also are for peace. We will camp beside you for to-night. We will not eat your meat. My young men will kill for us. We are glad to hear what you have to say about peace." Then he spoke to his following, and one went out into the storm, and the others went to work clearing away the snow and carrying in wood, and presently they had a big camp arranged within a few feet of ours.

In the meantime, through Joseph, I was holding intercourse with the two or three older ones who sat beside our fire. Soon their hunter came in, and six or seven followed him out. In an incredibly short time back they came loaded, and the whole crowd was in a short while busy roasting and eating the rich buffalo meat.

While all this was going on I could not help but reason as to why these men acted as they now did. A few months since, and they would have killed us. A few months hence, and they would do the same. Now the hard winter, the northerly trend of the buffalo, Maskepetoon's brave act—all this might and certainly did influence them; but so many do not think that far ahead of or around their present. Are these men moodish? Is this a peace mood? Are human passions subject to cycles? Is this the dip or the arch in the cycle influencing these men even against themselves to seek peace? How easily they could have killed us just now; forty to four, and fully half of these bigger than any of us. Do they want our guns and clothes, our blankets and ammunition? For less than this they have planned and killed many times ere this. What prevents them now? Is the hand of the Lord upon them? Has He a work for us to do? Are we immortal till that work is done, as this affects our present being? Ah! how fast one can think under pressure of circumstances.

I watched those men. I tried to look beyond the paint and the feathers and the manner of their actions. I mentally photographed them, in groups and individually, and thus the long hours dragged on, as the Sabbath evening had lost its rest for us. Then one of them, who had stuck close to our camp for hours, suddenly revealed the fact that he could speak Cree well. I was glad then that none of us had said anything that might in any way reflect on these men, for undoubtedly he had watched for this. After he had spoken I questioned him and answered his questioning until late at night.

When the Blackfeet began to stretch around the camp-fire, we did the same; but with the exception of Joseph (who *snored*) none of our company slept. At midnight we were astir, and harnessing our dogs, we took the meat down from our staging, and loaded our sleds, all the time watching our strange companions. There were three of us, in our party of four, who certainly in the letter carried out the first part of the injunction, "Watch and pray." Perhaps our prayer that night took the shape of constant watching.

We ate and watched, we lay down and watched; we got up and ate, harnessed our dogs, loaded our sleds, and prepared to start, watching all the time. The Blackfeet stirred as soon as we did, and about two hours and a half after midnight we each took our own course. Ours was straight for yonder northern mission. Our friends went I knew not whither.

With heavy loads we had to pick our way through the many hills. I sent Tommy ahead, my own veteran train was second in the line, then the pups. Joseph came after me with his and Tommy's trains, and Jim brought up the rear. Many an upset the alternately hard and soft drifts caused us, and very often Joseph and I had to strain in righting those heavy loads of frozen meat. The first two days we had no road, and our progress was slow. Then we struck a hunting trail from Maskepetoon's camp. This helped us, and following it we made better time. Then we left it and again went across country, leaving the camp to our left and coming out on the trail leading to the mission. We camped for the last night about forty-five miles from home. Starting out from this about two in the morning, we left Jim in the camp, and the last I saw of him for that trip was, as I drove my team away into the darkness he was running around catching his dogs. Before dark we were at the mission, and Jim came in sometime the next day.

Our arrival was hailed with satisfaction, for we brought with us meat, and this told of buffalo being within reach. Then the reports we brought of the Indians we had met were gratifying. Father and mother were delighted to hear about Maskepetoon and how he brought about peace, for the present at least. Then to have our little party together again, especially as Christmas was near, was extremely pleasing.

Our community at this time was made up of the mission party, the Hudson's Bay Company's postmaster and some employees, Mr. Connor and his son Jim. Besides these there were always some Indians camping near, coming and going. Peter had kept at the saw, and the lumber-pile was growing. Larsen was busy all the time making necessary furniture, and preparing material for the church which we hoped to build in the coming spring.

Thus the holidays came upon us in 1864 on the banks of the big Saskatchewan, far from the busy haunts of men, cut off from mails and telegrams and newspapers and a thousand other things men hold dear; yet in our isolation and frequent discomfort and privation we were happy. As father would now and then tell us, we were "path-finders" for multitudes to follow; we were foundation builders of empire; we were forerunners of a Christian civilization destined to hallow and bless many homes, and we were exalted with the dignity and honor of our position, and humbly thanked God for it.

Christmas found us all well, and our service, and the dinner and the games and drives which followed, though unique, were full of pleasant excitement. We had no organ or choir, but we all sang. We had no church, but the log shanty was as the vestibule of heaven. Our preacher was not robed in broadcloth, nor yet was he graced with linen collar, but his speech came with unction and power, and had in it the charm of a natural eloquence which stirred our hearts and stimulated our minds, and made us see before us grand ideals, towards which we felt we would fain strive.

We had no roast beef nor pumpkin pie, nor plates of tempting fruit, but we had buffalo boss and tongue, and beaver tail, and moose nose, and wild cat, and prairie chicken, and rabbits, and backfats, and pemmican. We were fairly lost in the variety of this one-class food. We had no flashing cutters nor gaudily harnessed horses, but we had fast and strong dog teams, and we improvised carioles and had some wild driving over hill and dale. We ran foot races and snowshoe and dog-train races. We played football and made this part of the Saskatchewan valley ring with our shouting and fun. Mr. Steinhauer came over and joined us on New Year's Day, and entered into the sports with all the ardor of youth. In the intervening days we made short trips for saw-logs and lumber, and helped to haul home hay and wood. In this way we combined pleasure and profit, and thoroughly enjoyed ourselves.

CHAPTER XXIII.

We set out with Maskepetoon for the Blackfoot camp—A wife for a target—Indian scouts—Nearing the Blackfeet—Our Indians don paint and feathers—A picture of the time and place—We enter the Blackfoot camp—Three Bulls—Buffalo Indians—Father describes eastern civilization—The Canadian Government's treatment of the Indians a revelation—I am taken by a war chief as a hostage—Mine host and his seven wives—Bloods and Piegans—I witness a great dance—We leave for home—A sprained ankle—Arrival at the mission.

THE year 1865 had barely started on its way when there came a courier from Maskepetoon to father, requesting him if possible to come out and go with Maskepetoon to the Blackfoot camp. The old chief desired to ratify the peace treaty, and to lengthen its days as much as possible. Father at once sent him word to make ready, and that he would be out in a few days. He decided to take Peter and me with him. Mother and the rest of our women folk were naturally very anxious about this trip into the camp of the dreaded enemy, but this did not prevent their helping to make us ready for the journey, and soon we were off, father in his cariole, with Maple and her pups hitched to it, Peter and I with our dog sleds carrying the provisions and camp equipment.

Starting early, travelling fast, and keeping at it late, we reached Maskepetoon's camp the second evening, and father and Peter worked late that night teaching and preaching. Next morning we were away with the chief and some forty of his warriors and head men. The weather was very cold, and the buffalo were now travelling north in large numbers, making their way into the Beaver Hills, and on to the Saskatchewan. It looked now as if we would not have to haul our meat from as long distances as last winter.

Father was the only one in the party with a cariole, and this he shared ever and anon with Maskepetoon. The rest of us were on foot, and as the snow was deep, except where the buffalo had trampled it down, our progress was slow. Other Indians, from camps situated at different points along the eastern and southern fringe of the Beaver Hills, joined us. Among these was a Blackfoot who was taking back a Cree wife. I took occasion to say to her, "Are you not afraid this peace may not last very long?" She merely laughed at my suggestion; but later on it came to pass that this same woman fell a victim to the Blackfoot she had taken as her husband. It is related of them that a few months after this, he and some others were gambling on a hill while the camp was moving past, and as this Cree woman came opposite the gamblers, her husband said to his companions, "See how I can shoot," and aiming at the woman, shot her dead in her tracks. An unfeeling laugh from the crowd followed the shocking tragedy.

As we journeyed the hunters of the party provided meat. The "cattle upon a thousand hills" were our storehouse, the hunters were our commissariat, and with sublime confidence in these we travelled on. The third day from Maskepetoon's lodges, we camped within a few miles of the Blackfeet, and early next morning our scouts were every little while bringing us news of the numbers and situation of the camp.

Hardy fellows those scouts were. We were moving at a brisk, quiet walk, but they must run on for miles, and then double on their tracks back to us. While away they must be invisible; they must see all that is to be seen, but remain unseen themselves. To do this they must take the contour of the country, note the condition of the sun and wind, be on the lookout for buffalo, coyotes, wolves, dogs, and ravens, crows, and other fowl. They must keep a constant lookout for contra scouting, and for this the nose and ear and eye and mind must be always alert. I say, to do this well, as many of these fellows can, requires the quickening of every sense. Then while doing all this, at times to make ten miles an hour on foot also requires a depth of lung and strength of limb and purpose of will which heredity and constant practice alone can give.

Our scouts that morning were like telegraph bulletins. We knew how the camp was arranged, and changed our course to suit this arrangement. We were told of the windings of the coulee, or valley, down which the Blackfeet lodges were standing. We were told of hunting parties that had gone out that morning; of the bands of horses, and how closely these were guarded; of the long strings of women and ponies, and dogs and *travois*, which were coming and going in various directions, packing wood to camp; all of which was literally true, for our scouts had been there and seen it all.

When close we stopped behind a bluff, while our men put on their visiting paint and dress material, and in a few minutes, with the small circular mirrors and ochre bags, our company was transfigured in appearance and colors. Bright colors in garments and on face made a wonderful change, and to my eye this was exceedingly fitting. The scene was in accord with itself; it was natural.

How often are we amused and then disgusted by merely made up scenes. Someone who has been just long enough in a new country to be made a victim of all the designing wags in it—who has just learned enough about Indians to make himself ridiculous every time he opens his mouth on the subject—will don the buckskins of a pioneer, or the costume of the aboriginal Indian, and pose for one or the other; but the whole thing is forced and unreal. Here we have the genuine article, and each factor in the picture is complete and natural and true: the sweep of the valley of the Battle River which slopes from our feet; the ranges of forest-dotted hills, climbing one above the other, from the river's brink even to the limit of our vision; the intersecting fields of snow-clad prairie, reflecting each in its turn the brilliant sunlight; the buffalo that here and there seem like ink dots on the vast ground of dazzling white that stretches far and wide; and the great solitude of primeval nature that broods over all. Then the curling heavenward of the smoke of our temporary fire, the athletic and well-proportioned physique of the men, their costumes and paint—I say all this was to my mind and eye, as I stood there and watched and waited that winter's day, as something just as it should be, belonging to the place and time.

But now the last feather is tied on, the last touch of vermilion is in its place, and we move on for another hour's quick tramp. A hushed excitement is apparent. This whole thing is yet a very uncertain quantity. Will success or disaster be the result? The most thoughtless in our party is somewhat checked by the anxiety of the moment.

In a few minutes the last scout will be in.

"Here he is!" We are about to come in sight and be within a few hundred yards of the camp. Maskepetoon and father step to the front side by side, as the chief would have it. Next come the standard bearers, and the Union Jack and the Hudson's Bay Company's flag are unfurled to the breeze; then the head men and chief warriors; then the young men and scouts. Peter and I bring up the rear with our dog-trains, which we have difficulty in keeping in their place—old Draffan has been ahead so often, he cannot understand his having to stay behind now.

The horse guards and wood carriers, and the children at play, were in full view of our advancing column, and at first there was a rushing of stock homewards, and a scrambling for the road by those engaged in hauling wood, while the children screamed and fled over the hill into the deep narrow valley in which the lodges were situated. An inexperienced person would never have thought that hundreds of tents, filled with warriors and women and children, were only a short distance from us; but presently up out of the valley came a swarm of men and boys, all armed and anxious. Then when the older ones recognized Maskepetoon, they began to shout "Mon-e-guh-ba-now!" and came to meet us gladly. As they came they fired their guns into the air, and our men did likewise, and sang as they marched, and in a few minutes we were on the brow of the hill and the Blackfoot camp lay at our feet.

Maskepetoon and father, with Peter and myself, were taken to the head chief's tent, and hospitably entertained in the style and manner peculiar to this people. Buffalo meat and dried berries constituted the food. The former was served either fresh or dry, or as pounded meat and grease, or as pemmican. The latter were either boiled or eaten dry. The vessels the food was served in were wooden, and the ladles it was dipped with were made of horn. Neither of these, so far as I could see, were ever washed. The cooks would cut up the meat for the guests as is done for small children among the white people. While in the Blackfoot camp we had no use for a knife, though we would have infinitely preferred to cut and carve our own food.

Father would quietly say, "Look the other way, John," and I would as quietly think, "If he can stand it, how much more can I."

Three Bulls, the chief in whose tent we were, was a tall, dignified old man. His war and hunting days were over, but there was a prestige in his manner and presence which spoke of a history for this man, and it was this no doubt which kept him in the commanding position he occupied. He had three wives living with him in his tent. These might be described as old, older, oldest. There were two handsome young men, his sons, evidently the children of different mothers. Both father and mothers were very proud of these superb specimens of physical manhood. The work of the camp was done by the chief's daughters-in-law and granddaughters, who came and went without noise or fuss in the discharge of their duties, while the trio of wives sat and sewed moccasins or played the role of hostesses.

These were thoroughly buffalo Indians. Without buffalo they would be helpless, and yet the whole nation did not own one. To look at them, and to hear them, one would feel as if they were the most independent of all men; yet the fact was they were the most dependent among men. Moccasins, mittens, leggings, shirts and robes— all buffalo. With the sinews of the buffalo they stitched and sewed these. Their lariats, bridle lines, stirrup-straps, girths and saddles were manufactured out of buffalo hide. Their women made scrapers out of the leg-bone for fleshing hides. The men fashioned knife-handles out of the bones, and the children made toboggans of the same. The horns served for spoons and powder flasks. In short, they lived and had their physical being in the buffalo. The Blackfoot word for buffalo in the mass in *enewh*. This same word in Cree means *man*. The Blackfoot word for buffalo bull is *stomach*, which in English means quite another thing. For the Blackfoot man the buffalo supplied the sole habiliment and the sole nutriment.

During our stay in the camp the women and children were frequently sent out of the chief's tent, and then the lodge would be packed with minor chiefs and headmen and warriors, who would listen to Maskepetoon and father. Lively discussions there took place on the benefits of peace among men. Father's descriptions of eastern civilization and Christianity were as strange revelations to these men. They listened, and wondered if these things could be true, so different were their experiences of white men from what father had to tell them of the conduct of our Government and of Christian men to the Indians in general. He told them of the many villages and tribes of Indians who were living in harmony and peace right in the midst of the white people, in the country he came from. One could see that most of these men were glad of the present respite, and yet there were some who chafed under the necessity of even a short intermission from their business of horse-stealing and scalp-taking.

There was one young war chief in camp who kept aloof from us, and as he had considerable influence and a large following, some anxiety was felt, both by our party and by the Blackfeet friendly to us. However, during the second evening of our stay, he came to the chief's tent, and it was announced that he was waiting outside. Our host gathered his robe around him and went out, and presently the proud young chieftain stepped in and took a seat beside us. Later on the old chief returned, and I enquired of Maskepetoon, "Why this unusual ceremony?" He told me that this young warrior chief was the son-in-law of the old man, and it was a rule of etiquette that the son-in-law should not come into a tent while his father-in-law was in it. So the old man had gone out until his son-in-law came in. Even here, as elsewhere, high-toned society must conform to rule.

This war chief said that he was not very anxious for peace, that war to him was like eating good fruit—he loved it; but as the others were favorable, he would join them for a while. Then turning to father, he said, "You must, if you are in earnest, let your son come to my tent and live with me while in our camp." Father asked me if I was willing, and I said, "Yes." So it was arranged that I should go; and presently the young chief signed to me to follow him, and we started for his tent.

It was dark as we wended our way in and out among the lodges in the windings of the valley, and it seemed to me that the dogs were without number; but a quiet, sharp word from my leader made them shrink away from us, and on we went for quite a distance. Presently we came to a large lodge, and entering this I found we were at home. The chief motioned me to a reclining couch of buffalo skins, and then began to speak to his wives and to a number of young men who seemed to be his dependents, and who were very obedient to his word. In the matter of wives he was four ahead of his father-in-law, having seven to own him lord, the last and youngest being the old chief's daughter.

Mine host—for I would rather consider him as such than my captor—was a tall, athletic fellow, about thirty-five years of age. He had a wild, wicked look about him, was quick and nervous in movement, and was, from appearance at any rate, a man not to be trifled with. His wives' ages, I should judge, ranged all the way from eighteen to thirty years, and there were several children. The lodge was the largest I had ever been in, necessitating at times the making of two distinct fires in it to keep us warm; for all this time the cold was severe, and our northern January weather was in full sway over this land. Some of the women untied a bundle of newly dressed robes, and made up for me a couch next to the chief's. They handed me some dried meat and berries, and eating a late supper, I turned in for the night. The isolation from the rest of our party was complete, and I could not repress a feeling of loneliness; but as father had arranged the affair of my being thus alone in this man's camp, I felt it was all right, and went to sleep.

Before daylight the camp was astir, and huge fires were burning in the centre of the lodge, but the keen cold was very apparent a few feet from these. As soon as I sat up in my couch one of the women brought me water in a wooden bowl for my morning ablutions, and I had my pocket-handkerchief to serve as a towel. Then they gave me for my breakfast boiled meat cut into small pieces. I longed for salt, but there was none.

All day strangers kept coming and going in

our tent. It seemed to me I was on exhibition. Once during the day my host signed to me to follow him, and we went out to the summit of a hill, where his band of horses were driven up by some young men who had them in charge, and I admired the number and quality of his stock. There must have been a hundred or more in the bunch, most of them, no doubt, the result of his stealings. Then we went back to the tent, and the day passed quietly away. In the evening a crowd of men occupied the space in our lodge, and much smoking and speech-making went on; but as I could catch a word only here and there, I did not understand what they said. As they talked and smoked I studied their faces and costumes, many of which were peculiar, inspiring me alternately with the feeling of dread and of curiosity. Everyone carried his weapons —bow and arrows, flint-lock gun, or war-club.

I could readily see that the idea of placing confidence in anyone had not as yet entered the minds of these men. Sometimes they became greatly excited, and as they frequently nodded or pointed to me, I could not but imagine all manner of trouble. Finally the crowd dispersed, and I was still alive and quite ready for the second supper mine hostesses served me with. I found that I was by heredity and practice a confirmed salt eater, and to be without it for a few meals was a hardship. There had been no communication since last night with any of our party. So far as I was concerned they might as well have been back at the Cree camp or our mission. However, when all was quiet I settled down into a sound sleep, undisturbed by even the dream of being scalped by dusky Blackfoot braves.

Long before daylight the big fires were blazing and crackling, faintly forcing back the fearful cold which had taken possession of the thin-walled and unfloored lodge during the few hours which the camp slept. I was up with the dawn trying to thaw myself out, but did not fully succeed until I had breakfasted. Another long day passed, much in the same way as the last, without any word from my party.

In the evening a number of Blood Indians arrived, and a dance was organized in our tent. This was my first meeting with any of these people. So far as I could see, they were the same as the Blackfeet, only of a more pronounced type—that is, the difference between them and the northern Indians was more marked. Proud arrogance and intense self-sufficiency seemed to speak out in their every word and action. One would think they were the aristocracy of the plains.

The meeting was more than a dance that

night—it was an experience meeting; for each one recited his deeds of daring, and acted in pantomime the approach, the ambush, the charge, and the shooting, stabbing, scalping, and horse taking of his past.

With frantic energy these men told of their various deeds of valor, and every now and then a comrade, a living witness, would shout, "It is true! I was there!" At this the crowd applauded, and the drums beat, while the next man sprang to his feet, and leaped, danced, whooped and sang; then when the drums ceased, he too would vaunt his feats of valor. All this was at first quite interesting to me, but as the hours went by, and it grew past midnight, I lost my interest, and wished the ball would break up. There seeming no immediate prospect of this, I stepped out, and running the risk of dogs and men, wended my way up the valley until I came to the old chief's tent, which I quietly entered, and raking the coals together made up a fire, as the night was bitterly cold. I saw that father and Peter were asleep, and Maskepetoon was stretched in his blanket between father and the fire; so I got down in front of Maskepetoon, and gradually crept under his blanket, until he gave it to me, after which he got up, made on more fire, and sat and smoked for the rest of the night, while I slept with a profound sense of rest and security beside my friends once more. Many a time in after days Maskepetoon would joke me about taking his blanket from him when in the Blackfoot camp.

From the time of our arrival here I had taken particular notice to a fine, manly young Blackfoot, who seemed to me to have an unusual interest in Maskepetoon. He would get as near to him as he could, and occasionally lay his hand on the chief's arm or shoulder, and name him "Mon-e-guh-ba-now," "the great chief," "the strong man," "the brave man," and Maskepetoon would laughingly turn him aside with a wave of his hand, but always in a kindly way. I wondered what could be the bond between these two, and at last I asked Maskepetoon who that young man was. "Why," said he, "he was the leader of the crowd that rushed at me and my grandchild a few weeks since. He and I are great friends now." The old man's brave act had won the enemy's heart.

The next day we started for home. We might have peace for three months or less. This was the impression on our minds. The people on both sides were too widely scattered and too independent of each other, and the range of country too big, to hope for any permanent peace under present conditions. In the meantime, even a short respite was something to be grateful for. Our route home was more direct, and we travelled much faster than in coming. The buffalo had been moving north, and in their progress trampled the snow for miles in many places, which helped us on our way. About the middle of the first afternoon I slipped on a lump of frozen snow and sprained my ankle, which made travelling for the rest of the evening a very painful matter, so that I was glad when we camped in the lee of a bluff of timber for the night. We had come a long distance, and it was pleasant to be in the open camp again.

After the work was done and our dogs fed, I took off my moccasin and found my ankle blue and much swollen. Through the long winter evening I sat there applying snow to the inflamed parts. This took down the swelling and assuaged the pain considerably; but I did not sleep much that night, and limped along with difficulty the next day. In spite of this, however, we reached our camp before night, and found that Muddy Bull had several animals staged ready for us. So father piled the camp equipment and our provisions into his cariole, while Peter and I took loads of meat, and with them reached the mission the second evening from Maskepetoon's camp, finding all well, and everybody wonderfully pleased to see us back. Peter resumed his work of lumber making, and I that of bringing in provisions.

CHAPTER XXIV.

We visit the Cree camp—I lose Maple and the pups—Find our Indian friends "pound-keeping"—The Indian buffalo pound—Consecrating the pound—Mr. Who-Brings-Them-In—Running the buffalo in—The herd safely coralled—Wholesale slaughter—Apportioning the hunt—*Finis*.

MY party for the next two months was made up of my old friend Joseph and a young Indian named Susa.

We started at once back to the Cree camp with four trains of dogs. On the second day out, near noon, we came to vast herds of buffalo, and my second train, composed of Maple and her pups, ran away with the buffalo. For a time we could see them, but soon they went out of sight in the distance, and leaving my old train of dogs to my men, I set out in pursuit of the runaway team. For miles I was able to track them; then the buffalo became so numerous ahead of me that all trace of the dogs was lost. As the course they ran nearly paralleled our road, I kept on until late, and after running some twenty miles, had to reluctantly give them up, and strike out to head off my men. We reached the Cree camp that night, and the Indians sympathized with me in my loss, and promised to keep on the lookout for the dogs. I felt the loss keenly, as the young dogs were developing handsomely, and were shaping to become "flyers." The camp we were now in was in their language engaged in "sitting by the place of bringing them in." This sentence of eight words in English is covered by one word of seven syllables in Cree, *Pe-tah-gionte-hon-uh-be-win.* This in short English would mean "pound - keeping." If the migration of the buffalo was west, then the mouth of the pound was west also. If this was north, the mouth of the pound was placed to the north, as it seemed to be the instinct of the buffalo when startled to run back in the direction whence he had recently come. In that direction he knew the great herds were roaming, and when startled he would fall back on these. Long before the white man came to the country, some Indians, more thoughtful than the rest, had noticed this, and concluded that a trap or corral might be built, wherein to catch them in larger numbers than they could be obtained by killing with the bow and arrows. Out of this happy thought was evolved the habit of building pounds, and killing buffalo wholesale in them.

In connection with this there was another evolution of men who became experts in bringing buffalo into the pound. These men professed to be aided by the "spirits," or "familiars," of whom they dreamt. The conjurers were not slow to make use of the "pound" business, and claimed that they could by their medicine make a pound lucky or unlucky as they pleased; all of which, as time went on, wove itself into the faith and tradition of the people, and gave these cunning fellows revenue and influence in the camps of their tribes. Ecclesiasticism and sacerdotalism were to the front, as they always are among ignorant and passively religious people. The situation of a pound was generally on the south or east side of a gently rising hill, the west or north side of this hill being prairie or open country, and the east or south side of it timber. In this timber, not far from the summit, the Cree pound was erected. This was done by chopping and clearing away the timber from a circular space—say one hundred, or one hundred and twenty-five feet in diameter. From this circle all the brush and trees, with the exception of one tree in the centre, were cleared out, and around this circle a strong fence of logs and brush was built, strong enough and high enough to hold the buffalo. At the entrance, which was made about twenty feet wide, a causeway, or sloping corduroy bridge, was built up of timber, so that there was a "jump off" into the pound of about three feet. The idea of a gate or bars had not dawned upon the people, as I will presently show. From the entrance on either side a strong brush and log fence was run out towards the north or west as was convenient. These lines of fence gradually diverged as they left the corral, until, at the end of a hundred yards or more, they were almost that distance apart. From the ends of the fence bundles of willows were placed on end at regular intervals for a mile or more, their outside terminals being fully a mile apart. These were called "watching waiters."

While the pound, the fence, and the "waiters" were being built and placed, the conjurers of the camp were making "strong medicine," wherewith to give luck and magnetism to the pound. For days and nights these medicine-makers and general dealers in the supernatural had pounded their drums and sang themselves hoarse; and now that the pound was ready for dedication, they organized a procession, and went on with the consecration of the pound and its accessories to the object in view. With solemn visages and in dignity of attitude, these priests of the old faith took their places at the head of the procession. With their medicine-bags in hand they stood like statues, while the rest formed in line, drummers and singers next to the priests. Then the whole camp, or as many as could attend, followed. At a signal the drums beat, the song was raised at the head, and then taken up all along the whole line, and to time they stepped away around the bluff, and turning into the fence, came down the lane, up over the causeway, and jumped into the pound. Turning to the left they marched around the circle of the pound, and then with short petitionary speeches, the conjurers proceeded to hang their medicine-bags on the limbs of the lone tree which stood in the centre. This done, the pound was dedicated, consecrated, and declared ready for work.

The next thing needed was buffalo. If these were within a few miles of camp, the man who had fat horses, and desired the tongues of the buffalo, be they many or few, that might be brought into the pound in one "fetch," would take his horse, ready saddled and bridled, to the tent of an expert at "bringing in," and say to him, "Here is my horse; now then go after them." Then the O-noh-che-buh-how, or "Who-Goes-After-Them," makes ready slowly and with dignity, assuming the air of one upon whom a grave responsibility is thrust, but who nevertheless is perfectly conscious that he is the one man to bear it, and perform the task entrusted to him. Thus he mounts the horse and rides forth.

This man is keenly watched by those who are on the lookout from the highest ground in the vicinity. The whole camp is in a flutter of excitement. Is the time propitious? Are the spirits friendly? Will the medicine work? Will "Who-Brings-Them-In" be wise in his handling of the buffalo? Is the pound properly located? Everybody is anxious about the new untried pound. As in the minds of other peoples the wide world over, here also was the strange mixing of reason and practice, and logic and superstition. But now those on the lookout are making signs, and it is shouted throughout the camp, "He has started a herd!" Again another sign. "The herd is a big one!" is the shout that electrifies every man, woman and child in the encampment; and while the thrill of this is still upon them, behold, there is another sign, and the joyful news rings forth: "They are coming straight!" Again the signal is given. "Make ready; to your places, O men!" and there is a movement by all the able-bodied men to the lines of fence which reach out from the door of the pound, where they place themselves opposite to one another. Behind the fence, and even beyond it, behind heaps of snow and brush, the men lie in waiting until the head of the herd passes them, when from each side they rise simultaneously and urge the buffalo on into the pound.

While all this is going on near the pound and in the camp, "Mr. Who-Brings-Them-In" is doing his level best with brain and voice and horse. Lay of country and direction of wind are noted. As he rode out he looked at the position of the sun. He pulled a little of the hair off his robe and let it go above his head to determine the exact direction of the wind. This he did on a hill, so that the movement of air would not be influenced by hills and valleys. When he sighted the buffalo he stopped, and lighting his pipe thought out the whole plan as well as he could, with the known quantities before him. For what was as yet unknown he held his pipe-stem skyward, and humbly petitioned the spirits to help him. Then he shook his pipe, and detaching the stem, he put both into his fire-bag, and remounting his horse started for the buffalo. If these were scattered he set out to bunch them. Riding slightly to windward and dismounting, he pulled a small bunch of dried grass out of his bosom, and chipping off a bit of punk he placed it on his flint. Striking this with his steel, when the punk caught fire he dropped it into a little nest he had prepared in the grass; then he waved this to and fro, and if the grass caught fire soon he was satisfied. If not, he took a few grains of powder from his horn and dropped them on the spark of fire on the punk, making a flame which speedily fired the grass. In a very little time the keen scenting buffalo would notice the tiny puff of smoke and move together.

Having bunched the buffalo, if they moved in the right direction he let them go and quietly watched them from a distance. If they went to one side, he headed them back either with a whiff of smoke as before, or by letting them catch a glimpse of himself. Thus he brings them within the long line of "watching waiters"; and now the herd is becoming excited, and begins to move rapidly. Riding close, he heads them on. If they rush too fast one way, he drops behind, and rides across their track the other way; and as he does this at a quick gallop, he utters a series of strange, queer cries which seem to be almost hypnotic in their influence, for the head of the bunch jumps his way as if in response to the weird cry. When the herd is going as he wants, he talks to them encouragingly: "That is right, O mother cow; you are doing well, keep right on; you will gladden many hearts, you will fill many stomachs, you will warm and cover many bodies." Then he

"Slapped-in-the-Face, take that one." (Page 282.)

would give his shrill cry, and as I have ridden beside these men when bringing in buffalo, it has seemed to me as if they had bridles in the mouths of the leaders of the herds, as these passively jumped to do their bidding. The man seemed transformed, energized, intensely consecrated to the object in view, and thus his spirit became masterful and strong in its purpose.

Now the lines of "watching waiters" are rapidly converging. The side to side rushes of the excited herd are becoming shorter, and follow one another in quick succession. Both man and buffalo are fast approaching the crucial point. It is now but two or three hundred yards to the end of the lines of brush and humanity. If the herd should break to either side before these are reached, the driver will be humiliated, the new pound made unlucky, and the whole camp sadly disappointed. "Who-Brings-Them-In" feels all this and makes supreme effort—throws his whole soul into the work. He calls, he urges, he petitions, he rides fearlessly and recklessly. Now the head of the herd is past the first of the line of concealed men, and these rise together, and others, and others, and on in a mad, wild rush sweep the deceived and thoroughly affrighted buffalo over the "jump off" and into the pound. "Who-Brings-Them-In" stays not for congratulations, but gallops to his tent, leaps from the horse, rushes in to his couch and flings himself on it, exhausted but triumphant. Perhaps that afternoon, to help him fully recover, some old friend will give him a Turkish bath.

I have described what happened when the buffalo were convenient to camp—say two or three hours' distant; but often they were a long distance away. Then the process was different. Another expert would start from camp on foot, and travel twenty, thirty or fifty miles into the north or west country, and at last, finding a suitable herd, he would slowly, by stratagem, by smoke and scent, work these toward the pound. Sometimes he would have to wait for hours for a "convenient season." Sometimes he would of necessity run for miles as fast as his strength and wind would permit, in order to turn the trend of movement into a more favorable direction for his object, and thus, after wearying days and nights, his bunch of buffalo would be sighted from the lookout, and "Who-Brings-Them-In" would ride forth and meet him, and take the herd in his turn, and the foot man would return to camp and rest.

What surprised me was that these men who went after buffalo and endured such physical hardship and nervous strain, did not receive any more than the rest in the partition of what buffalo might be brought into the pound. The man who owned the horse got the tongues, but those men who did the wonderful work of bringing in had the glory. Like the chiefs, who planned and lived for the people without any remuneration, these were the patriots of the camp.

But to return to my description of the pound. Soon the last buffalo was over the "jump off," and you may depend upon it, he was not far behind the rest, for the crowd of yelling Indians were at the heels of the herd. When all were in, the door or gap was suddenly filled by a solid line of men, who pulled their robes before them, and stood without a move as the mad herd settled into a gallop around the pound, always running as the medicine man had walked, and that was with the sun. In the meantime the pound was surrounded by the people of the camp, all rejoicing because of the success of the enterprise. Pound and medicine and men had all been blessed, and the hearts of the people were thankful.

Presently the twing of an arrow told that the work of slaughter had begun, and this was continued with arrow and flint-lock until all the large animals in the herd were dead. Then the boys were turned into the pound to fight the calves, and many a chase the calves gave them; sometimes driving the boys back up on the timber and brush of the walls of the pound. When all were dead, someone deputed for the duty would mount the back of a dead bull or big cow, and apportion the hunt.

"Slapped-in-the-Face, take that one."

"Hollow Back, you take that one."

"Who-is-Struck-in-the-Back, you have that one."

"Crooked Legs, there is yours."

"Red Bank, take that one."

"The-Man-Who-Strikes-the-Sun, here is yours."

"Bear's Child, this is for you."

"Wolf Teeth, cut that one up," etc.

In stentorian voice this man would divide the spoil, and soon the pound was full of men and women taking off the robes, cutting up the meat, and "packing" these to the tents. In a little while the new pound is left to the dogs, who in their turn hold high carnival among the refuse, fighting and feeding to the full. Not one buffalo is allowed to escape. The young and the poor must die with the strong and fat, for it is believed that if these were spared they would tell the rest, and so make it impossible to bring any more buffalo into a pound.

How this absurd idea was exploded, and how I found my lost dogs, and how we lived, and what we did and saw and experienced in the ensuing months and years, I hope to tell in a subsequent volume.

Forest, Lake and Prairie

TWENTY YEARS OF FRONTIER LIFE IN WESTERN CANADA, 1842-1862.

By JOHN McDOUGALL.

With 27 Full-Page Illustrations by J. E. Laughlin.

PRICE, $1.00.

Read the following comments:

"This is a true boy's book, and equals in stirring interest anything written by Kingston or Ballantyne. It ought to sell by the thousand."—Mrs. S. A. Curzon, in *Orillia Packet*.

"Possessed of an intimate acquaintance with all the varied aspects of frontier life, Mr. McDougall has produced a book that will delight the heart of every boy reader."—*Endeavor Herald*.

"There are many graphic descriptions of scenes in that vast fertile region in those early days when travelling was difficult and dangerous, but most fascinating to a youth of John McDougall's temperament and training. He lives those stirring times over again in his lively narrative, and relates his personal experiences with all the glow and vividness of an ardent, youthful hunter."—*Canadian Baptist*.

WILLIAM BRIGGS, Publisher, Toronto.

www.ingramcontent.com/pod-product-compliance
Lightning Source LLC
Chambersburg PA
CBHW030810230426
43667CB00008B/1150